KT-404-895

The Motor Impaired Child

The Motor Impaired Child

Myra Tingle

NFER-NELSON

Published by The NFER-NELSON Publishing Company Ltd.,
Darville House, 2 Oxford Road East,
Windsor, Berkshire SL4 1DF, England.

First published 1990
© 1990, Myra Tingle

Throughout the text, for ease of description only, the motor impaired child has been referred to as 'he' and the teacher as 'she'.

The views expressed are those of the author and not necessarily those of the Inner London Education Authority (ILEA).

British Library Cataloguing in Publication Data
Tingle, Myra
  The motor impaired child (Practical integration in education).
  1. England. Schools. Physically handicapped students. Integration
  I. Title   II. Series
  371.910942

  ISBN 0-7005-1249-7

Typeset by David John Services Ltd., Maidenhead
Printed in Great Britain by Billing & Sons Ltd, Worcester

ISBN 0 7005 1249 7
Code 8338 02 4

Contents

List of Figures

Dedication

To the children of Richard Cloudesley School, 1974–86

Acknowledgements

I should like to thank the teachers and non-teaching staff in ILEA schools who are helping children with a motor impairment to realize their potential in the mainstream school. It is from the difficulties and the triumphs of both teacher and taught that the text of this book has developed. I am grateful to my husband, Roger, for his encouragement during the sometimes difficult writing period and my thanks go also to our daughter, Emma, for her support and sense of humour.

Foreword

Mainstreaming, or integration, refers to the concept of educating children with special educational needs within the main body of the student population. The goal of integration is to reduce the stigma of attendance at a separate school, and is an attempt to avoid the negative identities and self-concepts formed by children who are separated from their peers. This theoretical assumption of a need for integration has been based on psychological and sociological studies that have demonstrated the harmful effects of low educational status on the development of a child's identity, expectations and performance. It is argued that by attendance at, and participation in, the life of the mainstream school, children with special educational needs will join the life of the community and will become full members of society.

The case for integration has been developed in many official reports and documents. For example, from the Ministry of Education (GB. MoE, 1954): 'No handicapped child should be sent to a special school who can satisfactorily be educated in an ordinary school.' And later from the Plowden Report (1967):

> Nearly all our witnesses supported the policy [the placement of physically disabled pupils in ordinary schools where possible] and we are in agreement with it. A handicapped child who will spend his life in the society of normal people and often in competition with them must learn to accept his disabilities and his differences...The necessary segregation of the handicapped is neither good for them or for those with whom they must associate. They should be in ordinary school wherever possible.

Again, from the report of a working party on children with special needs (Younghusband *et al.*, 1970):

> Ideally we should provide each child with the kinds of special help he needs and do so with the minimum degree of separation from his normal fellows and the minimum disturbance of family life...We start from the assertion that wherever possible they should be educated in ordinary school. But we have to consider deeply what we mean by 'wherever possible'...There are many children in special schools who could be educated in ordinary schools if resources were organised for them.

And from the Snowdon Working Party (1976):

> Integration for the disabled means a thousand things, it means the absense of segregation. It means social acceptance, it means being able to be treated like everybody else. It means the right to work, to go to cinemas, to enjoy outdoor sport, to have a family life, a social life and a love life, to contribute materially to the community, to have the usual

choices of association, movement and activity, to go on holiday to the usual places, to be educated up to University level with one's non-handicapped peers...

Over a quarter of a century ago, as a newly qualified occupational therapist, I was involved in re-integrating the disabled into the society in which they had grown up as 'normal' people, through a process or 'rehabilitation'. There were problems, of course — of physical access, of emotional adjustment and of public attitudes. I became disillusioned with a world full of prejudice, bias, narrow doorways and stairs. I reasoned that if all children grew up together, regardless of physical and intellectual ability, then they might more readily accept each other's similarities and differences and there might then be greater tolerance in later life.

After re-training as a teacher, I found myself working in a school for children with a physical disability. Here, the headteacher and staff were willing to initiate an integration programme with a local primary school. Later, as the newly appointed Director of the Centre for Motor and Associated Communication Handicap (CENMACH), and at a time when parents became free to choose integrated placements for their children, I was called upon to advise on writing aids suitable for the motor impaired child in the mainstream school. The text of this book is therefore based on 15 years' experience of the joys and disappointments of mainstream integration for the child with motor impairment. It is written from an integrationist point of view, which attempts to balance idealism and realism, and in illustration draws largely upon practical experience.

Children who survive with a physical disability are totally individual and we should not have preconceptions about their intellectual ability, emotional and physical state or potential to survive as independent citizens. Such children do not have learning difficulties or difficulties of physical access to a mainstream curriculum in the same way that they have, say, blue eyes or brown hair. The difficulties usually relate to the learning situation and the physical environment. It is hoped that this book will provide those working alongside children with motor impairment in the mainstream setting with a very little theory and a great many practical ideas. It aims to fuel their energy and their imagination so that the social climate of the classroom and then of the world outside can become the Utopia that has been drawn so hopefully with the pen over the last 30 years.

1 Introduction

Influences on current educational practice and provision

The Education Act of 1944 (GB. MoE, 1944) was a landmark of great significance for all children, including those with a handicapping condition. The principle of the Act was that education was to be available according to age, ability and aptitude within a broad concept that included concern for children's physical, moral and spiritual development. At this point, ten categories of handicap were defined and authorities were required to ascertain which children needed special education because of being affected by one or more of these handicapping conditions.

The development of special schools echoed the British philosophy and practice of classifying, sorting and grouping children. It was done so well that ordinary schools were free to narrow their own version of which children were acceptable. The special schools themselves were able to hold rigid views about which children they were equipped to take, and because many children did not show easily classifiable symptoms, often they and their parents were the victims of a long drawn-out debate amongst professionals about, first of all, which educational system, ordinary or special, and then, which type of special. This sorting-out process became increasingly controversial, and in May 1978 Mary Warnock (Warnock Report, 1978) wrote:

> The idea is deeply ingrained in educational thinking that there are two types of children, the handicapped and the non-handicapped . . . But the complexities of individual need are far greater than the dichotomy implies . . . we wish to see a more positive approach and we have adopted the concept of special educational need.

From 1974 to 1978, a Government Enquiry into Special Education had been conducted. The publication of the report *Special Educational Needs* (Warnock Report, 1978) by the Committee of Enquiry chaired by Lady Mary Warnock was a milestone in that it set out a new conceptual framework for special education. It established priorities and looked forward to significant changes in the ways in which special educational needs would be assessed and met.

The Warnock Committee estimated that one in six children would need some special provision at some point in their school life. Although such figures would be variable across classes, schools and geographical areas, they suggested that they should be used for planning purposes. They wished to abolish the system of classifying children by type of disability, a practice they considered to not only label each child but also each special school, so furthering the idea that children with the same disability required the same sort of educational provision. They maintained that only two categories, the blind and the deaf, required the provision of definite educational methods.

The Warnock Report, 20 years on

The 1981 Education Act (GB. DES, 1981) went some way towards implementing the recommendations in the Warnock Report (1978) but was introduced with little Government enthusiasm. Today, at a time of major and possibly traumatic changes in education, its philosophy and objectives are not much in evidence. But it would be wrong to assume that no progress has been made; greater awareness means that provision for children, their parents and involved professionals has improved since 1978.

Until 1983 a medical diagnosis was all that was legally necessary to determine whether a child needed special education. The Warnock Report endorsed the change to a multi-professional assessment, which altered the emphasis from 'treatment' to education. It recommended the abolition of categories of handicap and proposed that special educational needs should be individually assessed and met. The Report recognized a wider range of special educational needs that might arise at some time in the school lives of up to one in five/six children. It is hoped that these needs could be met in the mainstream school. It completed a process of making special education an integral part of the education system.

Many education authorities have accepted the need to make special education provision. We now have special educational need coordinators, and peripatetic and support teaching services. There are special units attached to mainstream schools and a growing number of children with 'statements' are now supported in mainstream classrooms. Individual special schools have developed links with local mainstream schools. Much has been done with limited resources.

Nowadays, special educational needs are met over a wider age span than ever before. Soon after birth, children have the attention of therapists, and later special nursery places are available. Young adults do not have to leave school until nearly 20 years old. Warnock introduced the concept of 'parents as partners' and the 1981 Education Act (GB. DES, 1981) was heralded as a 'Parents' Charter'. But, having been given more rights and responsibility in their child's education, it is evident that to use these rights effectively, to make their views heard both within special education and within the educational system as a whole, parents need help, either from 'wise' professionals or from within their own ranks. In London, the Parents' Campaign for Integrated Education later re-named Parents in Partnership is a powerful body with national support, which is working towards equal educational opportunities for children with special needs. (The address of this organization and of other cited organizations, companies, etc can be found in Appendix I).

The issue of integration has remained contentious and unresolved despite the considerable resources that have gone into researching its potential. In the summer of 1984 a report was commissioned on the efforts being made to meet special educational needs in a variety of settings within the Inner London area. A committee was set up, chaired by John Fish (former HMI for Special Education), and the ensuing report was entitled *Educational Opportunities for All?* (Fish, 1985). The question mark in the title implied that local provision was in danger of not delivering equal educational or social opportunities to a large proportion of pupils with special needs. It also implied that the means of improving this provision did not lie only in improving the special schools but that there was more to do in the wider educational environment. The Fish Report came up with wide-ranging plans for change and improvement and argued that Inner London should opt for full integration into mainstream of those pupils currently in special schools.

After public consultation over nine months, a policy was adopted which aimed to meet these needs but which would not be put into operation until there were adequate resources and only after proper consultation. The policy did not rule out integration for all, neither did it oppose it. It was accepted that for the foreseeable future, the special schools would still exist, although the balance between the different sorts of special education might change through more parents opting for their child to receive individual support in a mainstream setting.

By 1987, because of the increased demand from parents who were anxious to have their child educated in 'normal' school, numbers of mainstreamed children rose in Inner London schools to 1,200, representing 16 per cent of pupils with 'statements of special need'. But commitment to careful planning and the proper resourcing of integration is seriously threatened by the rate-capping of budgets, the break-up of the Inner London Education Authority (ILEA), and now the effects of the Educational Reform Act (1988). At the time of writing, one wonders just how many of the 16 per cent will be allowed to finish their education in the mainstream sector.

Looking forward

The National Curriculum (GB. DES, 1987) will test children at 7, 11, 14 and 16 years of age. For many children such tests will compound their difficulties, as these will be measures of achievement rather than a means of diagnosing need.

Since the Warnock Report (1978), special education has become identified with adding something extra to the lives of those with special needs. 'Statements of need' have been more positive and, in addition to educational support, the integrative approach of Warnock has been reflected in the current health and social services support, which might also be included in such statements as a legal right. Now it seems that statements may be used to exempt a child from or provide a child with less than the National Curriculum. Services such as the various therapies might not be forthcoming. Despite what is said to the contrary, the development of City Technology Colleges, grant-maintained schools and the increased role of school governors in determining admissions and expulsions will lead to all kinds of selection. This will mean that schools are less willing to accept, or hold on to, pupils who present them with the greatest challenge and who call for a greater proportion of resources.

The National Curriculum, with its emphasis upon competitive, vocational proficiency, does not give much weight to the creation of a community that will care for those who are disabled or disadvantaged.

2 Working Together

Implicit in the spirit of the 1981 Education Act (GB. DES, 1981) is the need for there to be a partnership between all those working with the child with special needs, so that by a 'joint endeavour' they will be able '. . . to discover and understand the nature of the difficulties and the needs of individual children'. As a result of the full assessment procedure and the child's 'statement of need', the mainstream teacher will need to learn how to work with a wide range of different people who will visit the class regularly, in order to 'treat' or 'support' or 'care for' the child. The special school teacher is accustomed to sometimes having more adults than children in her classroom, and to planning a timetable around those of the therapists. This interaction does not always go smoothly, even in a special school where classes are small and the demands of the curriculum are less intense; there is no reason at all why things should be any better in a mainstream setting. Mainstream teachers should not feel guilty if they sometimes resent the number of intrusions upon their teaching programmes; that feeling is understandable, especially if there has been no warning of imminent visitations. When this is the case, teachers are often angry because they would like nothing better than to be able to sit and talk to the visitor about the child but cannot because there is no one else to cover the class.

As a result of integration, teachers and therapists are having to work together in mainstream schools. It has to be admitted that sometimes this has proved very difficult and until recently, not much effort has been made to improve working relationships. The reason for poor cooperation could be that both teachers and therapists feel constrained by their roles. The therapist working within a medical approach is seen by the class teacher as an 'expert' who is required to 'prescribe' a remedy and effect a 'cure'. If this model is adhered to, then the teacher plays a passive role and the therapist feels that he or she is being denied curriculum support to effect and maintain therapy. Therapists may feel defensive of their specialized role and then vulnerable if asked to work publicly within a class. Teachers, on the other hand, may resent a therapist taking a child out of the class so that they cannot see what is being done. They may also feel that there is over-use of medical jargon.

It seems as if there is a need for combined training of therapists and teachers at some point in their professional training. This is not so unrealistic as it would seem and moves are afoot to make this possible. In the meantime, a more flexible, negotiated approach to the management of the child with special educational needs is required. Those working with a particular child need time set aside for discussion so that knowledge can be shared and areas of specialism allocated to individual members of 'the team', all within a spirit of collaboration and equal involvement in the overall management plan.

This chapter will consider the many different agencies with whom the teacher may have to work, explaining their particular roles and describing what the teacher might be able to expect for the child as a result of such collaboration.

The parents

One cannot consider a parent to be an 'agency', and all teachers are used to communicating with parents about their children. It may help, however, for the teacher to be aware of the possibly greater need for close links with the parent of a child with a motor impairment.

As soon as it is evident that the child is impaired in some way, the parents will have been exposed to a wide range of professionals whose job it is to alleviate the strains through practical or emotional support and advice. Some parents will have had good experiences of such relationships, which, it must be remembered, may have encroached upon some of the most personal aspects of their married and family life. Many, however, have not; for very good reasons they are fed up with their problems being exposed. They may make it very clear to the teacher that they don't want any interference, that they know that no one will ever make their child 'ordinary', and that all they want is for her to get on and educate him in as ordinary an environment as is possible.

The process of assessment

Parents' rights are gradually being written into the education system. In many ways, some parents of children with special educational needs may have more rights in terms of assessment and participation in educational decision-making than parents of children who do not have these needs. Circular 1/83 (GB. DES, 1983) elaborated, in real terms, upon the 1981 Education Act, and now 'assessment' is not regarded as a negative disability analysis of what is wrong. Instead it emphasizes parental participation and the professional perception of a child as a 'whole'.

Well-informed parents have the opportunity to influence what the professionals think about their children. They are able to get advice from the voluntary organizations, such as the Spastics Society, the Association for Spina Bifida and Hydrocephalus (ASBAH), or Parents in Partnership, who have taken on a major role in policy-making and advocacy to ensure that parents understand and get what is right for their child. They are able to bring to the assessment information that is not readily available to the professionals during their limited contact with a child. Sometimes parents don't realize just how much they do know and they certainly know more than the professionals give them credit for.

Any assessment that does not make full use of parents' knowledge will be incomplete and distorted. Yet often parents are afraid of upsetting professionals and of getting a reputation for not accepting their child's difficulties. If possible, the parents should be involved in their child's assessment well before the procedure begins. If difficulties in class are noticed, it may well be useful for the teacher to go and discuss this with the parent at home. Being able to see the child in his home environment and to chat about any difficulties over a cup of tea would be more thoughtful than bringing the subject up in a hurried five minutes at the start or finish of the school day. The parents might be encouraged to play a part in observing and recording specific behaviours; they may even have the use of a home video camera for this purpose. Their involvement in this way and the insights so gained will be most useful later when the issue of a full assessment might be raised.

Should a full assessment be decided upon, the headteacher, with the educational psychologist, will then need to provide the parents with adequate information about the process, its aims and possible outcomes. Professionals are provided with guidelines about completing a report in Annex 1 of Circular 1/83 (GB. DES, 1983), perhaps parents could be similarly helped. They may need to be made aware that some voluntary organizations, for example ASBAH, have already offered guidance to their members on parental submissions.

The parents need to know what will happen, the names, responsibilities and skills of the professionals involved, and how any decisions will be reached. They also need to know what their role in this will be and what their rights and obligations are. They should also be told about what services they can expect, both in the present and future. Openness at this juncture will enhance any further contact with professionals. Parents will also need to be able to discuss the assessment, not just in terms of what is known and written down, but also the unknowns, the uncertainties, the educated guesswork that might be in the minds of the professionals. Most parents would prefer frank, open reports so that they can get on and do the best for their child. To complete the process the parents will need time to talk to the class teacher and headteacher, and have information written for them in language they can understand. Many parents just cannot take in what is said to them in formal meetings. When the paediatrician first told them their child was not normal they most likely 'froze' and did not take everything in; the same may well be true for the formal assessment.

Physical care

When receiving a child with serious impairment into the mainstream class, the teacher must ensure that the parents tell her everything about his physical needs, abilities and limitations. Not only has she to organize her teaching programme around his care routine, she has also to ensure that, should his condition make him more vulnerable than the other children, he does not expose himself to potentially damaging situations.

Some parents will be very concerned about leaving their child at first. This is understandable and, whatever the teacher might feel, it is sometimes better to invite the parents to stay with the child until he gets used to the group and the group gets used to him. Not only can the teacher learn a great deal about care and handling, the parent will also be more at ease and will probably withdraw more quickly once the daily routine becomes familiar to them both and other responsibilities make demands upon limited time. They can always be called in to help with special events such as parties, plays and class outings, which may be difficult to conduct without additional hands.

Having any parent in class with their child can pose problems, and this is no different when the child has a motor impairment. The way in which the teacher handles the situation will influence its success. By giving the parents tasks to do with children other than their own, they will have a chance to get to know their child's class-mates, which may prove more difficult out of school when transport and mobility problems do not allow for easy socializing. They will also be able to make a more realistic assessment of their own child's abilities compared with those of his peers. Although this may not be easy for them at first, it will facilitate a more appropriate appraisal of his potential later.

Supporting therapeutic and educational programmes

If either a physiotherapist or occupational therapist is working with the child, it is quite possible that the parents have been instructed in how to carry on this support at home. In a similar way, they may be asked to participate in various attainment skills, such as handwriting practice, hearing the child read or spelling tests. It must be remembered that however keen they may be to help the child, there are only so many hours in a day, and they could be totally exhausted after caring for his physical needs as well as looking after the rest of the family. Demands upon the parents must be reasonable and take these factors into consideration.

If there is a problem over management of the child that depends upon consistent handling and shared expectations, then it is very important that both staff and parents cooperate to make the programme effective.

The medical and paramedical team

The school doctor and nurse

Many teachers complain that children with a motor impairment are placed in their classes without any information being shared concerning the nature of their condition. Although legislation has tried to ensure that 'labels' are dropped and that children's needs are described in more specific terms, it could be argued that by not describing the medical condition in more detail we are doing the child a disservice.

The Centre for Motor and Associated Communication Handicap (CEN-MACH) often receives completed referrals where the class or headteacher had not stated a disability but has used terms such as poor concentration, perceptual difficulties and poor motor control to describe the child's difficulties. A visit to assess the child reveals that he actually has spina bifida and hydrocephalus (see Chapter 3), wears below-knee callipers and walks with two sticks. First of all, the description of his difficulties only covers his learning difficulties and, for example, does not, should a typewriter be needed, warn us that portability may be a problem. In conversation with the class teacher one then learns that she has no idea that if he complains of a headache, this may need to be acted upon quickly, or that he will need extra to drink — and so it goes on. A recent course (pending accreditation by Thames Polytechnic, Diploma in Professional Studies in Education) on motor impairment, organized by CENMACH for London teachers, showed there was a real need for teachers to be aware of the aetiology (cause) of the childrens' conditions and to have time to talk to the medical profession about them. One could argue that this is because people tend to have a morbid interest in 'things medical' but our experience suggests that teachers are genuinely afraid of disability and need to know that their actions are not going to harm the child. They feel resentful when information is not shared despite the fact that they are expected to take daily charge of the child.

Although the school medical officer may only visit the school irregularly, the school nurse is a more frequent visitor. She is the representative of the Health Authority and provides a link between this, the school and the parents. The school nurse sees children regularly and checks vision, hearing, height, weight and general health. The nurse may also assist with health education programmes. Nurses are usually in full-time attendance in special schools for children with a physical disability but will not be so available to mainstream schools, even though many children with impairments are being educated there. This may mean that one of the members of staff has to take responsibility for first aid and other routine medical needs such as dressings and medication. It must be pointed out that staff cannot be made to take on this responsibility.

The school nurse in a special school is usually the person who disabled youngsters immediately turn to in times of personal difficulty. Nurses play an important pastoral role, which may be missing for the motor impaired youngster when he is in a mainstream school. At the moment we know of one young lad who is mainstreamed into a private boarding school. The staff are well aware of his disability and have made all the practical changes that are necessary. Recently they remarked that, unlike the other lads, he always arrived far too early for his daily tablets. This was obviously disconcerting for the school nurse who may have felt that she was always late! Perhaps the lad just wanted to talk and, having started his education in special school, saw the school nurse as someone in whom he could confide.

The physiotherapist

Physiotherapists are also employed by the Health Service. They are usually based in a hospital or a special school and then visit individual children in mainstream schools. The aim of treatment is to allow people with disabilities to achieve as normal a life as possible within the constraints of their impairment.

It is to the physiotherapist that staff should turn for advice on the correct use of walking aids, the provision of callipers, and the correct positioning of the child when working or playing. They will advise upon the most suitable method of mobility for the child and will ensure that he is not made to walk when, physically, he is not ready for this. They will also oversee his management of stairs and ramps (see Chapter 4), but the occupational therapist will most likely organize the provision of these. The physiotherapist will want the child to participate in physical education (PE) activities and will be able to advise on the best way for this to happen, possibly with adaptations to the exercises completed by the rest of the group. The therapist may ask that specific exercises should be included in his PE routines and that he stands in a 'frame' for periods of time in class. Physiotherapists may also advise on hand function, respiratory exercises for chest conditions, and will help with the correct use of inhalers and methods for clearing mucus from the chest.

Frequently the physiotherapist has been working with the child since he was small. She will know much about his personality and the parents' attitude to his condition. She will be able to give realistic information to the teacher about just what he can and cannot be expected to do. Sometimes the priorities of the physiotherapist and those of the teachers will conflict. The therapist may want the child to walk everywhere in the school, knowing that should he be allowed to use a wheelchair, there he will stay for the rest of his life. The teachers know how tired the child gets by the afternoon and feel that help with mobility will at least allow him to get through a day in an alert state. Both professionals have their points of view and the best interests, as they see it, for the child at heart. Obviously a compromise has to be reached.

The occupational therapist

Occupational therapists have only recently begun to develop their skills and expertise in the treatment of children. Growth in the number of children with minimal motor impairment now in mainstream schools has meant that occupational therapists are frequently asked to assess children whose gross and fine motor coordination is causing concern. The most commonly used test is the *Test of Motor Impairment* (TOMI; Stott *et al.*, 1984) although some therapists use the Aston Index (Newton and Thomson, 1982) or make up their own (see Chapter 5). After a full assessment, they will usually liaise with the class teacher, individual support teacher or classroom aide so that remedial programmes can be carried on in their absence. They may run groups for children with similar difficulties but from different schools during the school holidays.

Occupational therapists are primarily engaged in promoting independence and enabling the child with a motor impairment to play a full part in life both in and out of school. They will be concerned about the child becoming independent in the activities of daily living (using the toilet, dressing and eating). They will be able to advise on the need for aids and additional equipment, and on adaptations to buildings to allow the child full access to the curriculum activities and to all class and social areas.

Often it is the occupational therapist who is called in first to look at a child with poor handwriting. They may suggest handwriting practice with adapted pencil grips or writing surfaces (details in Chapter 5). They may suggest the use of a typewriter. Again, there could be a conflict of priorities here between the teacher and therapist. We find that therapists and parents may encourage the child to continue to handwrite because this is the 'norm'. Another reason for this is that they want the child to develop hand skills so that he can be proficient in other ways, feeding and dressing for example. From the teachers's point of view, the child is failing in an attainment skill and she wants him to be able to express his ideas in whatever fashion, hand- or type-written. Both points of view are entirely valid but compromise has to be reached so that the child's motivation to communicate through writing is not lost in the struggle to develop fine motor skill.

Occupational therapists also work with the parents and the child in the home and so the teacher has much to learn from taking the time to talk with them. They are also knowledgeable about perceptual motor difficulty and could advise on useful training programmes.

The speech therapist

Speech therapists are employed by the Health Authority and may treat a child in school or at home, or the child may attend a clinic. Therapy should be on a regular basis and for as long as the child needs it.

Such therapists are concerned with any problem that relates to spoken communication. They aim to help a child understand speech and to be able to express himself as fully as possible. If a child's language development is delayed or his articulation is poor, then therapy will usually be very effective. Some children may be unable to use speech effectively and, if this is so, then it is the therapist's task to decide upon and train the child in an alternative method of communication. This might involve the use of a chart (Blissymbolics; see Chapter 5), a signing system or a portable speech synthesizer.

If the child has difficulty eating, then the speech therapist will be able to advise on problems relating to biting, chewing and swallowing. If the child has trouble with excess saliva, she will be able to advise upon suitable strategies to reduce dribbling.

Effective integration needs effective cooperative working. Misconceptions concerning the roles and expectations of both teacher and therapist can lead to frustration and dissatisfaction with the progress made by the child. Because the development of spoken language is an area for which both speech therapist and teacher are seen to be responsible, it is very important that both set time aside to discuss the child's programme. It is best if the therapist is prepared to work within the integrative principle and does not withdraw the child from the class all the time. This way, she will understand more of what goes on at school, and later, when working with the child and parents, she will be able to make her treatment more effective.

Unfortunately, like most therapists, speech therapists are few and far between. We have met teachers who feel that a child should be receiving treatment but don't know how to go about referring the child. Obviously the first line of contact would be through the school medical officer but the College of Speech Therapists or the Association For All Speech Impaired Children (AFASIC) would be able to provide a school with their nearest point of contact.

Non-teaching staff

Non-teaching staff is just one title given to those invaluable people who are prepared to work alongside the teacher in the classroom without professional recognition and the level of remuneration that goes with it. Welfare assistants, teachers' aides, care staff, ancillaries — very often it is the particular 'title' that influences the relationship between the class teacher and the person who is being paid to support the child with a motor impairment within the mainstream class.

Welfare assistants are usually allocated to one child for a certain proportion of the school week. The length of time will depend upon the complexity of the child's physical difficulties, the generosity of the Local Education Authority, and whether there are other children in the school who need similar attention. She may be expected to deal with the toilet needs of the child, his medication, supervision at lunch and over break-time, and work alongside him in class. When asked to describe her role, the assistant may say that she is expected to back up and implement the curriculum that the teacher has decided upon for the child. The more cynical have been known to comment that they do whatever the teacher does not want to do.

Misunderstandings may occur if the assistant is asked to help out around the school when she feels that she should be working in the classroom or helping the child in other areas of his development, such as social and independence training.

The source of dissatisfaction can usually be narrowed down to the fact that the assistant feels her responsibilities are too great for such poor wages and difficult working conditions. Quite rightly, the issue of pay does need to be looked into by the employers. Another complaint is that training for the job is not freely available. Over 20 years ago, the Plowden Report (1967) not only recognized the importance of assistants in education generally but also made recommendations regarding their recruitment, numbers, role, training and careers. Plowden suggested a two-year college course with part of this time spent working in a school. The Warnock Report (1978) agreed that there was a need to train assistants but so far any training is limited to the odd day-course.

The assistants say that they would welcome formal training and acquiring more knowledge about the particular problems of the different conditions. They would like to know about the effects of medication, how to support the work of the therapists, and ideas to help the child cope with practical subjects and PE. They would like to know about the availability of resources and what methods they could use to improve concentration and increase the child's confidence. They have asked if an understanding of behaviour management techniques would be appropriate to their work.

It is very important that the headteacher should decide upon the job description for the assistant, taking into consideration the needs of the child and the environment they will be working in together. It must be remembered, though, that this will only be a guideline, for how can one quantify the time, understanding and flexibility that will be needed if the child is to have full access to the mainstream curriculum?

The value of the assistant will not only depend upon her abilities but also upon those of the class teacher to use this additional help in a constructive and creative way. It therefore extends the management skills and responsibilities of the teacher and, if used well, will allow her time for individual instruction, personal counselling and the development of lesson plans for the child and for any others who are causing concern. Communication will be the key to the success of this partnership. There should be some point during the day when both teacher and assistant can sit down and discuss plans for the next 24 hours. Failing this, a written daily diary or clear notices on the staff notice board concerning school events will be appreciated by the assistants.

Assistants should also be asked to report on the child's progress as and when this is required. Some may be asked to sit in on case conferences or annual reviews of the child's 'statement'.

The assistant will need to develop her responsibilities around the specific needs of the child. These in turn will depend upon the type and degree of disability present. A very useful booklet (Male and Ward, 1987), which comes highly recommended by assistants and teaching staff working in schools for children with a physical disability, is now available from the Royal Association for Disability and Rehabilitation (RADAR). The booklet outlines the role of the assistant and some of the functions they may be asked to carry out. It also aims to raise questions about general attitudes towards children and young people with physical difficulties, and to help both teaching staff and administrators to be aware of ways in which the assistant can contribute to the child's overall curriculum.

The individual support teacher

Although some children are allowed to have a welfare assistant and manage quite well with this level of support, others need to have periods of individual teaching. Unfortunately, individual support teachers (ISTs) often have to work with more than one child in a week, and these children may be at different schools. If this is the case, then the strain of travelling between schools and adapting to different teaching environments and styles can be very demanding for the IST. In turn, certain of the children will not have her support when they need it the most because individual timetables cannot be adapted to fit in with those of other schools. The child with a motor impairment may only get additional teaching when he is tired — in the afternoons or at the end of a week.

Ideally, where there is more than one child needing support in one school, the units of teacher time can be accumulated to equal those of a 'whole person'. This allows the teacher to fit in with the school timetable and provide the most appropriate support for all the children.

Support for a child with special educational needs is a relatively new concept in the primary school. In secondary education, the traditional role of the 'remedial' teacher was seen to be the assessment, diagnosis and teaching of clearly identified children, usually on a temporary withdrawal basis or in a special class. The new partnership role is broader and the boundaries are less clear. This then calls for a new set of skills on the part of both the support and the mainstream teacher, and for efficient management by the headteacher at primary level, or the senior teacher responsible for the timetable in a secondary school.

In the primary school, the IST will be seen more as 'belonging' to one particular child. At secondary level, although she may have been hired to support an individual child, she will become part of the special needs department and will need to fit into their particular way of working. Whatever the setting, the aim of support teaching in this context will be to allow the child with a motor impairment full access to the mainstream curriculum.

At primary level the child will need additional support with basic attainment skills. The IST could be responsible for improving handwriting or teaching keyboard familiarity. Some of her work may need to be carried out with the child withdrawn from the class, especially if he is very easily distracted, but it is her responsibility to ensure that he learns to become independent in class as soon as possible. In order to encourage his full integration she should arrange to teach the child within a small group. This will free the class teacher to give individual attention to the remaining children. She will need to liaise with the class teacher so that she can teach basic attainments within the context of the class curriculum and plan the necessary adaptations to equipment and materials that he may need in order to take part in practical activities. If the child does not have a welfare assistant, she may also have to support the child during PE, games, swimming, or on a class outing.

It may be that the teacher finds it difficult or strange to have a child with a physical disability in her class. She may prefer that the IST withdraws the child for as much time as possible. The support teacher will need to be constructive and encouraging towards the class teacher without threatening her colleague's self or professional esteem. She must also be prepared to stand firm and not allow the school to play just lip-service to the concept of integration.

The IST appointed to support a child at secondary level may find that special educational needs are seen to be the responsibility of the whole staff and not merely a specially appointed few. As such she will be expected to work with the child in class and across the curriculum. This assumes that she will be able to grasp the essentials of most subject areas and offer a range of alternative approaches, methods, strategies and resources to meet the child's specific needs. Her approach will have to be extremely sensitive to the needs of the teachers who may find threatening, both professionally and personally, not only the presence of an additional adult but also that of a child with a visible physical difficulty. For support to be successful, there must be time for the IST to liaise with all the child's subject teachers so that agreement can be reached on the content and sequence of lessons in advance. This will allow the IST to prepare for each lesson in such a way that the child will be able to read, understand and act upon the information presented as independently as possible. Without individual support, the subject teacher may not want to take responsibility for a motor impaired child in a practical lesson in case he damages himself or others.

After each lesson the IST will be able to check that the child has understood the task by involving him in discussion. She may also need to ensure that homework is recorded and completed on time and that project deadlines for the General Certificate of Secondary Education (GCSE) syllabus are adhered to. As many children with a physical difficulty will be eligible for special examination arrangements, it should be the responsibility of the IST, in liaison with his year or pastoral tutor and the member of staff responsible for the examinations, to make all the necessary arrangements well in advance.

In the context of the secondary school it is quite possible that it will be the child's IST who will know and understand him the best and will be a source of comfort to him as he approaches adolescence with a physical impairment. She will find herself involved in his intellectual, social and emotional development and may need to be able to share her perceptions of his difficulties with his parents or other staff members, especially if his behaviour is causing concern when she is not in school. As he approaches school-leaving age she will need to guide him to choose a realistic course of study or work experience, and to liaise with the specialist careers officer and the leaver's parents.

The school's attitude towards the child with a motor impairment will, in part, reflect the way in which the IST has been able to manage his integration into the mainstream curriculum. She will have 'set the tone' by effective management of his strengths and weaknesses, and will have allayed the fears that are so often the result of ignorance. In order to effect this change she may be required to plan and organize department or whole school-based in-service training (INSET, see p. 18) and any liaison between subject specialists and their counterparts in the school for children with a physical disability. If there are several children with different physical difficulties in the school, she may like to organize the publication of a little booklet written by the children about themselves. Such an introduction to how a physical difficulty might effect their performance in school, balanced by their expectations of a mainstream curriculum and their hopes and aspirations for the future, has been known to serve as an ice-breaker as well as a useful source of information to new staff. The importance of communication across subject specialisms and between staff as the child moves from one year to the next cannot be stressed enough.

The role of specialist teachers

The peripatetic teacher for the visually impaired

The peripatetic teacher will visit the school and want to liaise with both the child's class teacher, the IST and/or the welfare assistant. She will be able to explain the specific nature of the impairment and provide examples (via 'doctored' pictures and specially designed glasses) to illustrate what and how the child is actually seeing. From this it will be possible to tease out the implications for the preparation of learning materials and for general classroom management.

The IST may need to ask the adviser specific questions about teaching strategies, and mobility and social training. She will also need to find out about the provision and management of aids, some of which are highly sophisticated. She will need advice on examination arrangements for which the child may need to use specialized equipment, in addition to his typewriter.

If a child cannot see very well, his clumsiness will be exaggerated and he may annoy class-mates. Moving around the school he will not get the non-verbal feedback that is all part of informal communication. He won't be able to exchange the odd glance, grin or grimace and may not realize that anyone he knows is nearby, unless they bother to speak up. The peripatetic teacher will have experience of potential difficulties and will be able to advise staff or talk with other children about the importance of maintaining communication in a way that the child can understand and is able to respond to.

Should the child's sight deteriorate, the specialist teacher will be able to advise the staff on appropriate aids and adaptations to teaching method.

The peripatetic teacher for the hearing impaired

Like the specialist teacher for the visually impaired, the teacher for the hearing impaired will have had considerable experience of more profoundly handicapped children and is now using her skills to enable the impaired child to cope in the mainstream school.

She will want to work closely with the speech therapist, the class and support teachers and/or welfare assistant. As speech and language may be delayed because of hearing loss, she will need to discuss the development of these skills through suitable activities and exercises. If speech delay is prolonged, then she will advise alternative or augmentative forms of communication, such as signing or gesture. The management of hearing aids and the supply of batteries, and strategies for ensuring that the child understands when a signal such as the fire alarm goes off, are just some of the many invaluable pieces of practical information that she will be able to share with mainstream staff.

Within the teaching environment she will help the teacher to plan optimum listening conditions, teaching techniques, and the special arrangements for sitting school and public examinations. She will be able to suggest suitable links with further education establishments, work schemes and advice on careers.

Multidisciplinary in-service education

The integration of a child with a motor impairment into a mainstream school will mean that, possibly for the first time, teachers, therapists and other support services will be meeting on a regular basis under the same roof. The potential for both personal and professional growth is considerable and should not be overlooked. A programme of INSET that considers institutional organization and curriculum development from a multidisciplinary point of view could be extremely valuable to all involved, not least the children.

3 Physical Disability in Childhood

Impaired, disabled or handicapped

This chapter will consider the most common disabling conditions the teacher is likely to come across in the mainstream classroom. It is important to remember that each child is an individual. Both Ben and Emma may have 'Cerebral palsy' or 'Spina bifida' (defined in the next section) written in their medical notes but this does not mean to say that their physical difficulties or ability to learn will be the same. Upon meeting Ben and Emma, the teacher will need to decide whether they are 'impaired', 'disabled' or 'handicapped'. Any of these terms might apply in varying degrees to certain aspects of their daily life.

The importance of making a distinction between the terms impairment, disability and handicap has become greater as access to significant services has become dependent upon them. Professionals may hold different opinions over definitions and their usage, but they do agree that there is a need to categorize the disabled population, if only as an aid to interdisciplinary communication.

Impairment might effect locomotion, motor activities or sensory systems and be either medically based or psychological in origin. It is, essentially, an objective description of the site, nature and severity of loss of functional capacity. The degree of impairment can usually be measured or described — for example, by a sight or hearing test, the extent of muscle power, or the need to use a walking stick or typewriter.

We can say that a child has a *disability* when his impairment effects mobility, domestic routines or occupational and communication skills. Disability describes the impact of an impairment upon performance.

Finally, a *handicap* represents the more profound effects of impairments and disabilities upon the whole person and not just upon selected incapacities. It is a value judgement applied by others to that person on the basis of a failure to perform the customary social roles.

Impairment, disability and handicap form a continuum, ranging from objective descriptions of functional limitations to judgement of social disadvantage. To move from impairment to handicap is to move from symptoms to social role, and to move from objectivity to subjectivity.

Let us return to Ben and Emma, both of whom have cerebral palsy. Emma cannot walk; she is in a wheelchair and needs to use a typewriter for her written work; she is severely motor impaired. She is also disabled because she needs help to go to the toilet and to feed herself. In later life she will be handicapped because society does not provide many of the facilities needed by a woman with her degree of disability to live an independent life. Ben, on the other hand, has a weak left arm and limps slightly. His motor impairment should not prevent him from leading a reasonably 'normal' life.

Of course, he could also have perceptual difficulties that hinder the development of his writing skills. His learning disability will prove to be a problem
when he comes to take examinations and find a job; he may even appear to
be lacking in intelligence and his peers will say, 'Well, he is handicapped
after all!'

Whether or not the child with an impairment or a disability becomes a
handicapped adult will depend upon the resources available to him. It will
depend upon the response of society to his particular difficulties and the
lengths to which society is prepared to go to to minimize the mis-match between his needs and what is available to him. The mainstream curriculum in
a regular school building is a minefield of mis-matches — forewarned is
forearmed!

Making sense of a diagnosis

Although the final medical diagnosis of a motor difficulty may classify
children into groups, the outcomes of that diagnosis are so different for each
child that is impossible to generalize when considering the educational implications of each condition. What we do know is that physical difficulties
often bring with them a wide range of associated problems, of which any
one child will demonstrate a unique combination. To this end, each defined
'condition' has been matched against a table of areas for concern (Figure
2.1), each of which will be dealt with in greater detail later in the book. Information for this illustration has been collected from both medical and educational texts, and from personal experience; it is by no means a definitive
list. Care must be taken to read selectively, for once again we must stress
that not every child will have the full range of difficulties that may be associated with his particular condition.

Arthritis (Juvenile chronic arthritis; JCA)

DEFINITION

Arthritis may occur in a child as young as six weeks. The cause of the disease
is unknown but it is thought that the inflammation of the joints and sometimes other parts of the body is caused by abnormal antibodies in the blood.
The important difference between this condition in an adult and in a child is
that the child will most certainly be free of active disease after ten years of
age. The length of time that the child will remain ill will vary from months
to years. All therapy must be with the assumption that a permanent re-

Figure 2.1: Matching disabling conditions with areas of concern

Possible areas for concern

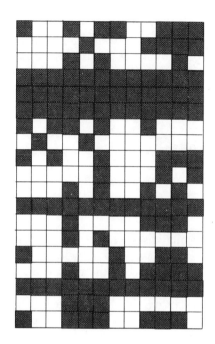

Behaviour
Diet
Epilepsy
Fatigue
Fine motor skill
Gross motor skill
Hearing
Heart condition
Hospitalization
Incontinence
Learning difficulty
Mobility
Immaturity
Reaction to noise
Pain
Self-care
Social skill
Speech disorder
Visual difficulty

Arthritis
Arthrogryposis
Brittle bones
Cerebral palsy
Freidreich's ataxia
Head injury
Loss of limb
Muscular dystrophy
Short stature
Spina bifida
Hydrocephalus
Spinal injury

 Indicates match

Conditions

mission will occur, and with good care very few children will be left with any real functional limitations.

ASSOCIATED DIFFICULTIES

Inflammation of the eye may lead to difficulties with vision. If the child is taking aspirin, there may be high-tone hearing loss, which disappears once the drug is stopped.

TREATMENT

There are no cures for JCA; the only treatment is to control the inflammation and the secondary effects until a natural remission occurs. Inflammation can be controlled by drugs and by providing rest for the joint and for the child as a whole. The effects of the inflammation — loss of motion in the joints — are treated by physiotherapy and, in a few cases, by surgery.

Arthrogryposis

DEFINITION

This is a congenital disease (present before or at birth) in which the child is born with stiff joints and weak muscles; the deformities are obvious at birth. The cause is unknown but the disease process begins in the developing foetus. It is not an hereditary condition, neither is it a deteriorating one. Depending upon severity, the child will be deformed and stiff with limited joint movement. Walking may or may not be possible but, because the trunk is normal, a wheelchair may be used if necessary.

ASSOCIATED DIFFICULTIES

There may be associated conditions, such as congenital heart disease, urinary tract abnormalities and respiratory (breathing) problems, but intelligence is normal and if properly motivated the child will capitalize on any opportunity to achieve independence.

TREATMENT

The aim is that the child will walk and be personally and economically independent as an adult. During early childhood, surgical treatment combined with plaster casts and braces may be used to combat deformities.

Brittle bones (osteogenesis imperfecta)

DEFINITION

Brittle bones are usually an inherited condition, resulting from an abnormality in the protein structure of the bones that causes them to break easily. In addition, the ligaments around the joints may be lax and the joints more mobile than normal. This is not, as once thought, the result of a calcium deficiency, and unfortunately there is not cure for it. If the condition is congenital, the baby is born with very short, deformed limbs, broken bones and a soft skull; survival is limited. In other children the condition appears later and is usually mild but still handicapping. There is no evidence of spatial or perceptual difficulty and the child should be encouraged to achieve academically.

TREATMENT

No known food or chemical has been found to affect the disease favourably. Frequent fractures may be treated by the insertion of steel rods into the long bones of the limbs. The main thing is to prevent deformities through therapy and to provide aids to independent living.

Cerebral palsy

DEFINITION

This is a non-progressive disorder of movement or posture that begins in childhood and is due to a malfunction of or damage to those parts of the brain that control movement. In some cases this damage may extend to other parts of the brain, so affecting vision, hearing and perceptual ability. The majority of children have this condition as a result of diseases and disturbances occurring during the mother's pregnancy or at birth (congenital cerebral palsy). In a few instances, it may be the result of a brain tumour or haemorrhage (bleeding) or skull fracture.

TYPES OF MOVEMENT DISORDER

1. *Spasticity.* The limb muscle is tight, and with sudden attempted movement or stretching the muscle contracts strongly. As the child grows, the spastic muscle becomes shorter with resulting deformities of the limbs, pelvis and spine.
2. *Athetosis.* The limbs make involuntary, purposeless movements; the muscles are normal and not spastic. Purposeful movements are contorted and uncontrolled.
3. *Ataxia.* This is a lack of balance sensation and of position sense in space, together with uncoordinated movement. Such children walk as if they were sailors on a rolling ship at sea. Hand–eye coordination is poor and they fall easily.
4. *Tremor.* A shakiness of the limb involved, often increased when an attempt is made to use that limb (intention tremor).
5. *Mixed.* Usually, these children have all four limbs affected and have both spasticity and athetosis.

TYPES OF LIMB INVOLVEMENT

Monoplegia — one limb.
Hemiplegia — upper and lower limb of same side.
Paraplegia — lower limbs only.
Diplegia — major involvement of lower limbs, upper limbs less involved.
Triplegia — three limbs involved, one upper and both lower.
Quadriplegia — major involvement of all four limbs.

The motor involvement and the limb involvement are specified in the diagnosis; for example, cerebral palsy, spastic hemiplegia.

ASSOCIATED DIFFICULTIES

1. *Oral/dental.* Some children may find it difficult to swallow and so feeding is a problem. Dribbling may continue into adult life and teeth need constant attention.
2. *Speech.* Some speech or language defect is present in 50 per cent of the children. This may be due to paralysis or poor coordination of the speech muscles (*dysarthria*). Affected children may not be able to organize and select speech (*dyspraxia*) and some children have no speech (*aphasia*).

3. *Hearing.* Hearing loss is most common in athetosis; a very small number of children are affected.
4. *Vision.* Many affected children are far-sighted; some find it difficult to look upwards; some have a squint. Overall, about 20 per cent of children have a visual defect.
5. *Sensory problems.* Loss of shape and texture sensation in the hand is well documented especially in spastic hemiplegia.
6. *Epilepsy.* The possibility of epilepsy (see next section) is more common with spastic cerebral palsy (for example, hemiplegia). About 25 per cent of the children are affected.
7. *Perceptual and visual motor difficulty.* The child will complain that he cannot make his hand copy what his eye can see. He may not 'see' things in a distorted way but rather in an immature way — there is a developmental lag.
8. *Low intellectual ability.* A significant percentage of children with cerebral palsy will not be very bright; research estimates at least 75 per cent, but the remaining 25 per cent can be of average or above average intelligence. Very often the most physically disabled (athetoid quadriplegics) are the most clever. Ataxia is most likely to be associated with mental handicap.

TREATMENT

Prospects of improvement depend greatly upon an estimate of the degree of brain damage and intellectual ability; also upon the severity of the movement disorder and the availability of early medical, paramedical and educational intervention. Treatment is through physiotherapy, speech therapy, occupational therapy, bracing, orthopaedic surgery and drugs. It is important that all agencies work together so that the child is able to reach his potential educationally, socially and in personal independence.

Microcomputer technology now plays a major part in this process.

Freidreich's ataxia

DEFINITION

This is a rare inherited disease of the central nervous system (the brain and spinal cord); it is genetic in origin and will cause progressive deterioration in coordination and muscle control. The condition can become evident at any time between 5 and 20 years of age.

ASSOCIATED DIFFICULTIES

Poor balance of the limbs and trunk: at first the child will appear clumsy but later will start to fall frequently, or a wide-based 'drunken' walk may develop. Poor, fine motor control, often with a definite tremor, will affect eating and handwriting, and speech may become slurred. There may be poor circulation and weakness of the heart that can cause palpitations and diabetes (see next section).

TREATMENT

Most children will be able to complete junior school without mobility aids but they will need physiotherapy regularly to teach stability in movement and to maintain mobility for as long as is possible. To maintain personal independence and to improve impaired speech and eating, the services of an occupational and a speech therapist will be necessary.

Head injury

DEFINITION

Head injuries are usually the result of trauma (road traffic accidents, sports, and so on. The effects of the injury range widely from severe physical disability and associated brain damage to minimal change in the child's intellectual processes. The term 'head injury' will not in itself give any indication of present or future ability and no two children with such injury will be affected in the same way.

Evidence suggests that the longer the child remains unconscious after the accident, the less likely he is to make a complete recovery. After recovery from coma (deep loss of consciousness), no improvement in general independence after 18 months suggests that the child may remain severely handicapped for the rest of his life.

ASSOCIATED DIFFICULTIES

After the accident the child is usually unconscious, and upon waking will have no memory of what happened. Memory loss or post-traumatic amnesia (PTA) can last for some time, and if the child returns to school during this period, he may still be disorientated and confused. There may also be physical impairment, vision and hearing problems, epilepsy, lack of ability to use and understand language, and behaviour problems as he learns to adjust to his changed circumstances.

TREATMENT

This will depend upon the degree of disability. In addition to medical and paramedical support there will be a need to support the family through the litigation to obtain damages, and for experienced counsellors to work with the child, family and school during the phase of adjustment.

Loss of limb

DEFINITION

The absence of a limb may be congenital or acquired. A *congenital amputation* means that the child was born without a limb or part of a limb. The cause of this is a failure of the foetal limb bud to develop during the first months of pregnancy, for example through the effects of the drug thalidomide. Acquired amputation means that the child has lost the limb in part, or completely, through an accident or by surgery, possibly for a malignant bone tumour.

ASSOCIATED DIFFICULTIES

The child's intellectual ability will be within the normal range but his functional abilities will depend upon the site of the amputation. Children born with a limb deficiency have some sensitivity in the remaining section of the limb and are able to use this to their advantage; children who lose a limb later in life understandably find adjustment difficult and need encouragement to make the most of artificial limbs (prostheses).

TREATMENT

The provision of artificial limbs and training in their use is the total treatment. The absence of both upper and lower limbs (*amelia* presents severe problems that can only be solved with special electrical prostheses and other devices. Liaison between family, therapists and school will ensure that the child reaches his potential in personal independence.

Muscular dystrophy

DEFINITION

This is a progressive weakness of all the muscles due to muscle fibre being replaced by fat and fibrous tissue; this degenerative change is technically known as a dystrophy. It is a disease that can affect both sexes but the most common type, *Duchenne muscular dystrophy*, is carried through the female line and affects only boys. The child appears normal at birth but sometimes walking is delayed and will appear 'clumsy'. Soon the child will develop a protruding stomach and a 'sway back' from early weakness of the muscles of the abdominal wall. Weakness progresses slowly with times of remission and times when deterioration is rapid. Prolonged bed-rest for any reason seems to make things worse. Although each child is different, most boys will be in a wheelchair before their teens and life expectancy is limited. Two years ago researchers discovered the elusive gene that causes Duchenne, and then found also that a certain protein was missing. At last, there is hope that a treatment may be found in the foreseeable future.

ASSOCIATED DIFFICULTIES

Intellectual ability is within the normal range and, if the school has total wheelchair access, there is no reason why the child should not receive all his education in mainstream education. Fatigue, the need for physiotherapy and hydrotherapy (treatment in water) and the difficulties of emotional adjustment to a changing state may mean that he decides to move to the more sheltered environment of special education. Child and family will need help in adjusting to the possibility of an early death.

TREATMENT

No effective treatment exists although vitamin supplements and special diets have been tried. Physiotherapy is necessary to inhibit contractures of the joints and in the early stages various braces may be used to keep the legs, arms and trunk in the normal position. Very often children need to wear night splints. Surgical treatment is helpful at times to correct early deformities of the lower limbs and to maintain walking. All who work with the child must live in the hope that a cure will be found within his lifetime and should believe that however short a child's life it can still be filled with challenges, enjoyment and creativity and not be a life of treatment alone.

SPINAL MUSCULAR ATROPHY

There are some conditions that affect muscle strength but do not follow the same pattern as a dystrophy and so an early death is not expected. However, as the child grows, the muscles do not have the strength to move the extra weight and so the child appears to be growing weaker. The educational implications will therefore be similar to those of a dystrophy.

Short stature

DEFINITION

There are two categories, proportionate and disproportionate short stature, and both may be due to a number of different medical conditions. *Proportionate short stature* is when the growth of the body as a whole is restricted and, in addition, the child may suffer hormonal disorders and disease of the kidneys and heart. If detected early enough, this condition can be treated and the child will reach normal height. *Disproportionate short stature* is the result of a genetic abnormality of bone and cartilage development; it cannot be treated.

ASSOCIATED DIFFICULTIES

Orthopaedic problems from abnormalities in bone growth will affect mobility; the child may have bow legs or a club foot; he may be obese. Some children may have difficulty with hearing or sight. Girls who have Turner's syndrome (a genetic abnormality involving glandular problems, short stature and mental deficiency) may have associated learning difficulties.

The greatest problem for all concerned is that a person who is child-size has to fit into an adult-size environment, and this means adaptations to furniture and difficulty with general mobility.

TREATMENT

Surgery is sometimes necessary to correct deformities. All who are involved with the child should have normal expectations for academic and social development. It is easy to treat a child in a manner appropriate to his size rather than his age. Swimming is a good form of exercise but advice should be taken before the child is exposed to physical activity because this may put too much stress on abnormal joints and the spine.

Spina bifida and hydrocephalus

These two conditions commonly occur together but may also occur independently. For ease of explanation, they are dealt with separately.

Myelomeningocele, meningocele, spina bifida

DEFINITION

Myelomeningocele. An out-pouching of the spinal cord (see p. 92) through the back of the bony vertebral column (spine).

Meningocele. Almost the same as myelomeningocele except that the out-pouching consists only of the coverings of the spinal cord (the meninges).

Spina bifida occulta. A failure of formation of the backmost arches of the vertebrae (spine bones). The bony defect is covered by skin; there is no out-pouching (*occulta* = hidden). For unknown reasons the neural tube fails to develop completely and close in the first 30 days of pregnancy. It is a condition more common in females, who are also more likely to be severely affected.

ASSOCIATED DIFFICULTIES

The physical consequences depend upon the spinal level of the lesion and the amount of damage to the spinal cord.

Paralysis of the trunk and lower limbs. The extent of weak or absent muscle function depends upon the level of the damage to the spinal cord. If this is at or above the twelfth thoracic vertebra, almost total paralysis will occur. If it is at the third lumbar vertebral level, the trunk muscles are spared and parts of the hip and thigh muscles are preserved, but leg, foot and ankle muscle functions are absent.

Partial paralysis. This leads to muscle imbalance and resulting bony deformities; that is, dislocation of the hip, club foot, severe flat feet, spinal curvatures.

Loss of sensation. The skin does not respond to pain, heat and touch; the extent of this change coincides with the level of the damage to the spinal cord. Serious skin problems can develop (burns and pressure sores). Children have to be taught to look for skin damage and shift their position frequently.

Incontinence. Because the damage is nearly always above the level of the major nerve supply to the bowel and the bladder, there will be paralysis of the muscles that control urination and defaecation. The child will thus be doubly incontinent and will have to be taught to express himself, empty urinary appliances and possibly handle self-catheterization (see Training in Personal Independence below). Failure to do this may cause renal (kidney) failure due to back-pressure from the bladder. Much can be done by regularity in visiting the toilet and a suitable diet.

TREATMENT

1. Surgical closure of the spinal defect to prevent infection. This does not necessarily reduce the paralysis.
2. Early bracing with callipers if the damage is below the twelfth thoracic vertebra; this will enable the child to learn to walk with crutches. If the damage is minimal he may only need sticks or below-knee callipers. With damage above the twelfth vertebra, wheelchair mobility will be the norm.
3. Surgery, as appropriate, to reduce and prevent deformity and to deal with the problems of permanent incontinence.

Hydrocephalus

DEFINITION

Circulation of cerebrospinal fluid through the brain is hindered by a malformation at the base of the brain (the Arnold–Chiari malformation). The ventricles (chambers) within the brain become distended and would eventually compress cells and nerve fibres. The condition is apparent at birth in two-thirds of affected infants. The result, if this is not corrected quickly after birth, is mental handicap, and sometimes spastic paralysis of the lower limbs and epilepsy. Hydrocephalus is often associated with other congenital anomalies such as hare-lip and spina bifida.

ASSOCIATED DIFFICULTIES

Even if action is immediately taken, the child with both spina bifida and hydrocephalus will have more learning difficulties than if spina bifida was the only problem. There is also a likelihood of a squint developing. Problems associated with the actual 'shunt' (see Treatment below) are many, and should the child show any of the following symptoms, medical help should be sought: *vomiting, drowsiness, headache, clumsy walk* [that is, more clumsy than usual], *irritability, loss of concentration, loss of consciousness.*

TREATMENT

Because the cerebrospinal fluid in which the brain and spinal cord are suspended is almost identical to blood plasma, it is possible to drain off the excess fluid into the blood stream. This is done by inserting a 'shunt' — a pressure-sensitive, non-return valve under the skin on the side of the head.

Because the child grows and because the shunt can get blocked or disconnected there will probably have to be repeated shunt surgery. Infections in the shunt and in the urinary tract will be treated with antibiotics.

As cerebellar development is most rapid during the first 18 months of life, it is at this time that parents and pre-school support should work on the development of hand–eye skills (the cerebellum is the part of the brain involved in muscle coordination and balance). To treat the child as a 'normal' baby is not good enough (Rosenbaum *et al.*, 1975).

The hydrocephalic child is usually very sociable; he is good at what is called 'cocktail party chatter'. His conversation, however, has very little to do with the social context in which it occurs; it is not participatory and it does not give room for the other person. Parents often have difficulty in coming to terms with the fact that their apparently 'bright' child has wide-ranging learning difficulties and possibly a degree of mental handicap.

Spinal injuries

DEFINITION

Traumatic damage to the child's back is usually the result of a road accident, a fall whilst playing, or an injury sustained when involved in sport. Very rarely, damage can also occur as a result of an infection. Through the inter-connected spine bones (vertebrae) runs the soft spinal cord of nerve bundles running to and from the brain; damage to this cord will result in loss of movement and feeling (paralysis) below the level of the injury. In general, the higher up the spine the damage, the more the child's body will be affected. Thus damage to the neck leads to *tetraplegia/quadraplegia* — all four limbs are affected; damage to the back leads to *paraplegia* — the legs are affected.

ASSOCIATED DIFFICULTIES

In *tetraplegia* it is quite likely that the child will need to be on a ventilator to aid his breathing. He will not be in control of any bodily functions apart from eating and limited speech. In *paraplegia* the child will have limited mobility or need to use a wheelchair. He may have no control over bladder or bowel. Because of lack of sensation and poor circulation, it is easy to damage the skin and the wounds will take a long time to heal. Whatever the degree of disability, the child and his family will need to come to terms with a different way of living.

TREATMENT

After an accident the child should not be moved until skilled medical help has arrived. Incorrect transportation of an injured body can sometimes make the difference between an incomplete (spinal) injury that will recover and a complete injury that will not. After hospitalization, rehabilitation starts as soon as possible; this will involve physiotherapy and occupational therapy and a return to school with the continued support of the therapists, electronic communication aids, counselling services and careers advice.

Associated disabilities

A child with a motor impairment very often has an associated medical condition or sensory difficulty to cope with. Hidden handicaps often affect the child's educational progress more than his motor difficulty.

Asthma

This is one of the most common chronic diseases of all schoolchildren and can be an additional problem for a child with a physical disability. It can start at any age and is spasmodic. The child will become breathless and begin to wheeze as the bronchial tubes tighten, the linings of the tubes become swollen and there is an increase of mucus in the lungs. Air can still be taken in but the child has difficulty in getting it out. He will become tense and frightened as his chest becomes more inflated. Minor attacks may go unnoticed but if the attack is more severe, stay calm and make sure the child uses his medication. If this does not bring relief, call medical help.

Most children will carry and know how to use an inhaler which dispenses drugs (see also p. 52) that will relax the bronchial muscles and help to restore normal breathing. Some children, because of anxiety, tend to use their inhalers too much. This should not be encouraged but it will not harm the child and he may become more anxious if it is taken away from him. Some children may take medicines in tablet or syrup form as an alternative.

Asthma attacks can be provoked by several factors, such as anxiety or excitement, excessive exercise (especially where this involves sudden changes of temperature), allergic reactions to pollen, animals or certain foods, and coughs and colds.

Children with asthma may use this as an excuse not to do games and PE. Their reluctance may be due to a real fear of precipitating another attack and so it is best to check with their parents to see how genuine this is. The child may be able to take a tablet or use the inhaler about 20 minutes before the lesson to provide relief. Swimming in a heated pool is a very good form of exercise. There are no learning difficulties that are the direct result of having asthma; however, general poor health may reduce the ability to learn.

Diabetes

This is an inherited condition in which the body is unable to make normal use of glucose (the blood sugar) because it cannot make the hormone insulin properly, which is necessary for energy to be released from glucose. Treatment is to inject carefully regulated and regular does of insulin. It sometimes takes a while to reach the careful balance of hormone needed to reduce the risk of future diabetic complications, such as blindness and heart disease, but once this is achieved there is no reason why the schoolchild should not take part in a full curriculum. Either the parent or the child will see to the injection in the morning and there should be no need to repeat this during the school day.

However, diet and exercise during the day may affect the level of glucose in the blood. If the child is late for a meal or takes more exercise than usual, this may cause the level of glucose in the blood to drop (*hypoglycaemia*) and his diabetes will be out of control. The signs to look for are *headache, dizziness, nausea, vomiting*, profuse *sweating*, and *cold hands and feet*; the child may become very *irritable*. This all happens very quickly but can be stopped by giving the child fruit juice with added sugar, sugar lumps or special sweets. The difference in the child will be seen within a few minutes.

If too little insulin has been taken, the blood glucose level will be too high (*hyperglycaemia*). This is a potentially dangerous situation and if not treated quickly the child could pass into a coma and die. The onset of symptoms is gradual: they include *tiredness, abnormal thirst* and *hunger*, and passing *large amounts of urine*; the skin feels dry and warm.

There is no reason why a child with diabetes should not take a full part in the school curriculum, including games and PE. However, it is wise to allow him additional snacks both before and after excess exercise.

Epilepsy

Epilepsy can be the result of brain damage or fever and so can be associated with physical disability. It is a passing disturbance of brain function in which there can be periods of unconsciousness (generalized tonic–clonic seizure, previously called 'grand mal'), or 'absences' (previously called 'petit mal'), which are mild seizures rather like day-dreaming. Epilepsy is not a specific disease but more a symptom of a disorder in the central nervous system. It cannot be cured but can be controlled in the majority of cases by a careful regimen of a drug(s) that suits the child. Factors that may precipitate an attack include a failure to take the drugs at a regular time, stress or fatigue, and sometimes flickering lights. If properly adjusted, computer screens should not present a problem, neither should TV screens as long as the child sits at least two metres (six feet) away from them.

If a child in your class is known to be epileptic, it is essential that you discuss with his parents what to look out for and what to do should a fit occur. Most parents are happy to cooperate but some may prefer to play down the issue in the fear that their child will be stigmatized. If this is the case you will need to seek medical advice. You may be asked to record, in detail, the events before, during and after a seizure, facts which will help the child's doctor in managing the condition.

Sometimes a child with major epilepsy will have a warning (an 'aura') such as giddiness, noises in the head, or a tingling sensation, and will be able to get himself into a safe situation before he becomes unconscious. The teacher will need to keep calm and reassure the rest of the class, who may be frightened by his convulsions. The child may also wet or dirty himself and this will need to be handled sensitively. As long as the child is not in a position where he can damage himself, it is best to leave him until his movements have stopped, and then roll him onto his side and comfort him as he wakes up. If a seizure lasts for longer than 15 minutes, medical help must be called. The child may also want to sleep for a while but should be encouraged to come back to class as soon as he feels able.

Major fits obviously interrupt learning; what is not so often realized is the cumulative effect of epileptic 'absences'. They happen so quickly and often go unnoticed — concentration is affected and the teacher may find that, as a result, the child has missed or not understood fundamental points. Drugs may cause drowsiness and affect concentration and the child's ability to learn. During the early stages of treatment or if a new drug is being tried out, he may exhibit either aggressive or extremely passive behaviour.

Heart conditions

It is possible that a motor impairment may be further complicated by a heart defect. In congenital heart disease the most common defect is 'hole in the heart', where there is an abnormal communication between two chambers of the heart. With luck the hole will be small and will close naturally or at least become much smaller. If this is the case, no treatment is necessary and by the time the child starts school he should be able to take part in the full curriculum. If treatment is necessary, this is usually carried out when the child is very small and again will not affect schooling. Some children may be vulnerable to endocarditis, an infection of the tissue lining the heart and its valves, which may be caused by bacteria entering the bloodstream from infected teeth and gums, ear or skin infections, or childhood ailments. Thus dental care is very important, and the child must have the full immunization programme available to all children.

There are no learning difficulties directly associated with heart conditions but if the circulation is poor there will be a limited oxygen supply and this may lead to sudden fatigue, which will reduce the child's ability to learn. If surgery is ultimately needed, time away from school will be a problem; and where PE, swimming and games are concerned, it is necessary to check with the parents and the child's doctor to ensure that the level of activity expected of him is within his ability.

Hearing impairment

Hearing loss on its own constitutes a major disability. By cutting the child off from a world of sound it reduces his ability to learn and communicate through language. The consequences of this for other areas of development are considerable. If a child with a motor impairment has an associated hearing loss the teacher should seek out appropriate information and support from those who are specifically trained in the education of the deaf.

Damage to the ear may result in hearing loss of any one of the following types. *Conductive deafness* results from an obstruction or malformation in any part of the outer or middle ear. The most common problem is 'glue ear', the result of an infection in the middle ear, which causes partial or temporary deafness in about 20 per cent of children at any one time. Appropriate treatment (draining the fluid by suction and fitting a grommet — a tiny ventilation tube) will improve hearing but the condition may recur intermittently.

Some children will *sensorineural deafness*, which may be present from birth because of a genetic abnormality or because the mother contracted German measles (rubella) or some other viral infection during the first three months of her pregnancy. Prematurity or a difficult birth resulting in an oxygen deficiency may also do damage. During childhood, viral infections, such as measles, mumps and meningitis, may be a cause of a sensorineural deafness that is the result of a malfunction in the inner ear or auditory nerve and prevents the perception of certain sounds. The deafness may be helped by wearing a hearing aid. It is possible to suffer from a mix of conductive and sensorineural hearing loss.

Hearing loss is measured by loudness (in decibels [dB]) and by pitch (frequency), and the test is carried out using an audiometer, an instrument that will produce an audiogram (a graph of hearing deficiency). As a rough guide, a loss of 25 dB is similar to having a bad cold. When an audiogram indicates a loss of around 30 to 35 dB it is likely that the child will have some difficulty in hearing quietly spoken speech. From 35 to 45 dB there will be difficulty hearing normal speech; if there is a loss of 60 dB the child may be aware of speech sounds without the use of amplification but it is unlikely that he will be able to interpret them. By 80 dB the child cannot hear loud speech without amplification, and with a loss of 120 dB he may hear only grossly distorted speech patterns. The audiogram will give important pointers to which speech sounds a child may have difficulty hearing (*s* and *f*, for example, may not be perceived at all), and will indicate the most suitable type of hearing aid. It must be remembered that the results of the test will only be one small clue to the child's ability to understand speech. Inner ear damage affects different children in different ways, and much will depend upon age of onset and diagnosis, past experience, and the child's ability to use residual hearing well.

What is important is to be aware that some degree of hearing loss may be present, and that however mild this may be it could still have serious educational implications for the child who is already coping with both physical and specific learning difficulties. Because these difficulties may be more obvious, the fact that the child has a hearing loss may have gone undetected and so it is important for the teacher to determine whether lack of attention and delayed language or poor sentence construction, for example, are due to the primary disability or to undetected hearing loss. The school doctor will be able to arrange a hearing assessment and then, if appropriate, sources of support would be the speech therapist and the peripatetic teachers of the deaf, who work mainly in mainstream schools and also support parents of pre-school children with hearing impairment.

Speech and language difficulties

The reception class teacher will be familiar with the odd child who comes to school for the first time with poor speech. This may be nothing more than the inability to utter a few sounds correctly; or the child may whisper, stutter, or be quite unintelligible. If this is the case, not only will the teacher find it difficult to understand him, it may also become clear that the child has a minimal motor impairment with associated difficulty in writing and reading.

Most children start to make sounds and use simple words between the ages of 12 and 18 months. By four or five years they have mastered most of the sounds they hear around them. If this does not happen, they may be described as being 'language delayed' and they do, usually, 'grow out of it'. If language is still unintelligible at six or seven years of age, then the child will be described as having a speech or language disorder. It is not always easy to distinguish between speech delay and speech disorder.

Speech difficulties that persist are usually associated with another impairment such as poor hearing, motor deficiency or learning difficulties. Serious problems like these are usually described by therapists as *phonological disorders, dysarthria* or *dyspraxia*. To help the class teacher to understand these medical terms the following summaries may prove useful.

PHONOLOGICAL DIFFICULTIES

These are thought to result from an impairment in the ability to establish the rules of how sounds, particularly consonants, are used. The child may eventually produce a good range of sounds and will be able to initiate these in isolation or at the start of words but will find it very difficult to establish those at the ends. He may also find it difficult to notice the difference between words that start with the same sound but are entirely different; for example, doll, dog or dot. He may not realize that words can have different meanings with only one sound changed, and may also be unable to sequence words correctly. Children with phonological difficulties may more accurately be said to have a language disorder. They usually respond well to speech therapy.

DYSARTHRIA

This means that there are physical reasons why a child cannot speak. There may be a disorder in the speech structures — the lips, tongue, teeth and soft palate — such as a cleft palate, or in their movements as is the case in cerebral palsy or other trauma to the brain. The child's voice is slow, nasal or slurred. Speech therapy will teach strategies to improve articulation but the child will always have some residual difficulties and there comes a point when therapy is no longer useful.

ARTICULATORY DYSPRAXIA

This means that the child finds it difficult to imitate and reproduce speech sounds even though the necessary muscles are not paralysed or weak. The more the child talks the more difficult he is to understand. The child appears to be unable to plan and organize the movements of the tongue and lips to produce sounds and to sequence these correctly in words. The child is aware of his difficulty and this inhibits the normal development of his language. Progress in speech therapy is usually slow but in the end treatment gets results. Some children have both phonological and dyspraxic difficulties.

APHASIA

Some children have no speech at all and yet can hear normally and are of average intelligence. Access to the mainstream curriculum will depend greatly upon the degree of their physical disability and upon specialist advice concerning a suitable form of augmentative or alternative communication.

Visual difficulties

Many children who are motor impaired also need to wear glasses. As with hearing loss, when a child has associated specific learning difficulties it is very difficult to decide whether it is the brain that is not making the right connections (perceptual difficulty) or whether they just cannot see what they are supposed to do (difficulty with the physical mechanisms of sight). Perceptual difficulties will be dealt with in more depth in Chapter 6 but it may be helpful here to point out what to look out for if poor vision is suspected, and then to describe how vision is measured and how to understand and respond to the results of the test.

The eyes of a child who is having problems seeing may be cloudy, swollen or inflamed and may water frequently. There may be erratic or excessive movements of the head and eyes, and he may complain frequently of having a headache. In class he may blink a lot or frown and screw his eyes up when trying to see what is on the board. He may prefer to copy from a neighbour rather than from the board and have to move closer than the other children when something is being demonstrated. Should suspicions be aroused, then the school doctor will be able to arrange for a specialist eye test.

The most usual test for measuring vision is the Snellen test. This is just one of the charts with which we are all familiar that start with one large letter at the top, the letters gradually getting smaller towards the bottom of the card. If the child has 6/6 vision this is normal; 6/24 means a slight to moderate impairment — the child can read at 6 metres what a child with normal sight could read at 24 metres. Using this example, 6/60 vision equals a moderate impairment and 3/60 a severe impairment; both may be enough to register that child as partially sighted. Children with less than 3/60 vision may be registered as blind. Educationally blind means that the child's main method of learning is through tactile material, for example, Braille.

Glasses may be prescribed for various reasons but it must be noted that for some children with visual difficulties they may not be appropriate. If the child has near-sight (*myopia*) he will need to wear them for distance vision, looking at the chalkboard, games, visits to the theatre or the museum. If long-sight (*hypermetropia*) is the problem he will need glasses for reading and close work. At all times glasses should be kept clean, unscratched and in good repair, and there may be a need to keep a spare pair in school for those times when they are forgotten and left at home or on the bus or in the taxi!

The educational implications of a visual defect are considerable and even a minimal impairment needs to be thought about in terms of teaching strategies and materials. This will be covered in more detail later in Chapter 5.

Training in personal independence and self care

The motor impaired child in the mainstream school is usually there because he himself, his parents or other caring adults consider that this is the best place for him to receive his education. It is assumed that he will grow up to be an independent adult with a job, his own home and possibly a family. However, the very fact that he has a motor impairment may prevent him from achieving this goal because the impairment may have associated difficulties that will affect his ability to care for his personal needs. If a person cannot dress, wash, eat and go to the toilet independently, setting up home alone, getting to and from work and being socially acceptable whilst at work will be difficult if not impossible.

An important aspect of any child's education is that which develops personal independence, and the mainstream teacher needs to keep this high on her list of priorities when planning a motor impaired child's programme. Other school staff should also be aware of what is planned and have a realistic idea of what the child can and cannot do and what he needs to learn to do. The cooperation of the parents should be sought, though this may prove difficult especially if the child has been recently damaged, say in a road traffic accident. Their natural reaction will be to do everything for him and to shield him from further trauma. It is important to liaise with the therapists and any medical staff in planning for independence because they will be able to advise on self-care routines, which are important and provide practical ideas for training.

Various aspects of self care are considered in detail here. It is important for the school to be aware of these so that suitable arrangements can be made to allow the child with a motor impairment full access to school buildings and the curriculum. It may be thought that such details should be kept 'within the home' and that they are not the province of the class teacher. But full access to the curriculum also means full access to all outside school activities, such as field trips and school journeys. Here the class teacher will find herself *in locoparentis* and will need to be able to plan for suitable support to make this possible.

Toilet training

If the child has no neurological reason why he cannot become toilet trained, then it is reasonable to expect that he will be dry (apart from the odd accident) before starting school. The child with small stature may need to attend the toilet more frequently due to having a smaller bladder but there is no other physical condition (apart from a urinary infection) that suggests a greater need to be absent from the classroom. Some children who have their own classroom aide may use 'needing the toilet' as an excuse to get away from work; they enjoy the individual attention and the social encounters en route. But, once there, a child with cerebral palsy may need to take more time and this should be allowed for.

PROBLEMS OF ACCESS

The motor impaired child may know that he needs the toilet but be unable to get there in time or, once there, be unable to reach the toilet or cope with his clothes. The child with short stature or with limb abnormalities may need to have a small stool left beside the toilet and the wash basin, the towel rail may need to be lower, and if the flush has an old-fashioned chain this will need to be lengthened. Foreshortened upper limbs may make personal cleanliness a problem but there are aids available from occupational therapists that will solve this. Likewise they will be able to advise on suitable fastenings to make management of clothes easier.

If the school is intending to take in a child in a wheelchair or one who is on crutches, who will both need much more privacy, then it will be necessary to adapt a toilet to make it a single unit. It will need space for a wheelchair beside the lavatory pan, washing facilities and a changing bench that is adjustable in height (to ease transfer sideways from a chair and then to be at a suitable height for the care staff to work against without damaging their backs). Some children may need specially adapted toilet seats and handrails but both could be free-standing. A small extractor fan will clear unpleasant odours without the need for aerosol sprays. A toilet adaptation to suit the full range of disability may be more expensive initially but more practical and economic in the long run. Advice from the occupational therapist should be sought before going ahead with any major structural changes.

INCONTINENCE

A social taboo surrounds the very real fact that at some time in our life we will all wet or dirty ourselves without meaning or wanting to. Incontinence that is the result of damage to the nerves and muscles controlling these bodily functions cannot be cured but it can be managed. It will most surely be a major problem for the child who is paralysed from the waist down because of a spina bifida or trauma to the spinal cord. An associated difficulty will be personal hygiene, which is essential for social acceptance.

Management of bladder incontinence. The child will need to empty his bladder fully three or four times a day. To do this he will need to drink regularly [five to six pints (about three litres) of fluid] and learn how to produce a reflex action in his bladder to persuade it to empty at regular times.

Of course each child is different but the sooner such training is started and he finds out how best to do this for himself the better. If special outings are planned, when this would prove difficult to go to the toilet, it is acceptable to cut down temporarily on liquid intake.

Some children may never be able to achieve control of the bladder in this way. When they are young they will wear disposable nappies and plastic pants. The problem of disposing of the used pads can be a very real one and this will need to be sorted out before the child joins the school. Most special schools have a machine in the toilet which heat-seals black plastic bags; the bags and their contents are then collected separately and incinerated. Most local authorities operate special collection arrangements for waste of this nature.

As children get older it is better for all concerned if they can learn to cope with some type of urinary appliance. Boys have fewer problems than girls; they are able to wear a specially fitted penile bag that then drains into a second bag strapped to the leg, totally invisible under a pair of trousers. Both boys and girls can wear *in-dwelling catheters*. These are fine tubes fitted directly into the bladder and held in place there by a small balloon. Urine drains down the tube into a collection bag. Some catheters can remain in position for up to three weeks but most need to be removed two or three times a week; parents can usually manage this but strict hygiene is crucial to prevent an infection entering the bladder. Care must also be taken to ensure that the catheter does not become kinked or crushed, so preventing free drainage of urine into the bag. This method of coping with incontinence may sound frightening but it does allow the child to be independent when attending the toilet because he can empty his own bag with little or no help at all.

Some children will have a permanent artificial diversion of the bladder that opens onto the stomach wall. The diversion is called an *ileal loop* and the opening is called a *stoma*. Urine is discharged directly into a changeable plastic bag. The child must have the ability to master the system and must have access to hot water and privacy. In the long term adolescents may prefer this method, which is more sexually and socially attractive than incontinence pads, but each case will need to be considered medically as well as socially before the operation takes place.

Management of bowel incontinence. This is usually less of a problem than urinary incontinence as it is usual to have only one bowel movement a day. But failure to control bowel movements can cause social problems and limit social outings. It is possible to achieve an acceptable level of control if the child sticks to a routine such as warm water first thing in the morning, sometimes combined with glycerine suppositories in order to stimulate a bowel movement in about 10 to 20 minutes. Attention should also be paid to the diet so that a natural stimulant can be identified and taken regularly. Long-term use of laxatives is not recommended. For medical reasons some children may have a *colostomy*, which is the bowel equivalent of the ileal loop described above.

Kidney and bladder infections. Any child who is incontinent is likely to be prone to urinary infections. If urine is allowed to collect in the distended bladder it will become stagnant and infected. There will be back pressure on the kidneys, which will impede their functioning. Infections may also be introduced into the bladder through lack of cleanliness when changing catheters. Symptoms to watch for are those of a *cold, fever, blocked nose, perspiration, fever* and *vomiting*. Treatment with antibiotics will only have a short-term effect and, in the end, prevention is better than cure. The child must drink frequently and make sure that the bladder is emptied completely.

MENSTRUATION

Puberty effects all teenage girls, and in certain conditions (particularly spina bifida), the onset is advanced by some years so that some girls at primary school may have to deal with menstruation as well as incontinence. The wheelchair girl is no different to any other when it comes to the problems associated with the monthly circle, so aches and pains should not be allowed to get out of proportion and emphasis should be on normality and acceptance, supported by full explanations of what is happening and what is to be expected. Life in a wheelchair is difficult enough without creating additional 'problems'; however, if periods are heavy they will prove a practical problem for a girl who has to sit all day, so medical advice may be sought and the condition treated with hormones.

PERSONAL HYGIENE

However careful one is, accidents are bound to happen and the incontinent child is going to live in fear of public ridicule and social isolation because he smells. Hot, stuffy classrooms do not help and so it is important that the child has additional changes of clothes available, and that clothes are washed in such a way as to eliminate bacteria and smell. Plastic pants are best treated with a disinfectant such as Napisan, which will clean thoroughly without changing the nature of the plastic.

ASBAH (the Association for Spina Bifida and Hydrocephalus) run a series of training courses for youngsters who need training in personal independence skills and a very useful book *Understanding Incontinence* by Dorothy Mandelstam (1989) is available from the Disabled Living Foundation.

Dressing

All youngsters want to wear clothes that are in fashion, and many parents make great efforts to look for and buy clothes that come up to their own and their child's expectations. Unfortunately, what is chosen is often expensive and impractical. This imposes additional limitations upon an already 'limited' child. He is not allowed to crawl around or get involved in activities that will make him 'dirty'. He may be fed to prevent food from staining his clothes. He may find that the clothes are so tight or have such difficult fastenings that what independence he has is still further limited. Furthermore, the patience of the most dedicated care staff will be stretched when changing a child who is incontinent and wearing callipers is further complicated by the need to get slim-fitting jeans on and off.

With imagination, clothes can be bought and if necessary adapted to be both fashionable and practical. A few basic rules need to be followed: avoid back openings, especially those with buttons, which will be most uncomfortable for a child who sits for most of the day; avoid, or exchange for Velcro, zips or buttons that may cause pressure sores or that are difficult to do up or undo because of poor, fine motor skill. Tops and bottoms that can be bought separately are ideal; they are easy to get on and off and the child may need one size for his top half and another for the bottom. If blood circulation is a problem, then clothes should not be tight-fitting; even the ribbed band of a sock could restrict the blood flow and cause damage to the skin. Children who get very hot (those using crutches or manipulating a wheelchair) should wear natural rather than synthetic fibres to reduce body sweat. Clothes should be warm and light-weight so that the child does not become chilled but still has freedom of movement.

Obviously parents are responsible for the purchase of a child's clothes but tactful suggestions initiate change and encourage practical thoughts on the subject. Is it sensible to buy brand-new clothes for everyday use when the child will be spending most of his playtime crawling on the floor, or when callipers will soon wear holes in them? What is so wrong with buying from jumble sales or the local charity shop? On a busy day in any school, special or mainstream, having to fight with difficult clothing is guaranteed to make staff bad-tempered. Unfortunately, this is often apparent to the child, who is made to be more conscious than ever that he is a 'problem' to his carers. The Disabled Living Foundation (1981) publish a comprehensive book, *Dressmaking for the Disabled*, which provides ideas for adaptations and alterations that are well within the capabilities of most people.

Occupational therapists will also be able to advise on gadgets to help a child to dress (dressing sticks and sock gutters) and will organize training sessions in this. The child with spatial and sequencing problems will have difficulty in organizing himself: clothes may go on back to front or inside out; they may dress themselves in the wrong order. Therapy can teach the child to plan his routine to minimize these difficulties. It sometimes helps if the child can wear jumpers with patterns on the front only and if coloured tags are sewn into the seams so that he can identify the arm holes. Pockets need to be accessible. Even such basic things as the height of the child's peg in the school cloakroom will make all the difference to his ability to be independent upon arrival at school, at playtime and at home time.

Mealtimes

EATING AND DRINKING

These activities are sometimes a major problem for the child with poor control over his facial and throat muscles. Poor control may be the result of disordered movement patterns as in cerebral palsy; it may also be due to muscle weakness, the result of muscular dystrophy or a condition such as Friedreich's ataxia.

For such a child, opening the mouth, chewing and swallowing will be difficult to coordinate; he may therefore dribble out of the corner of his mouth whilst drinking. He may have poor grip and hand control, so further complicating the process. The child's face, jersey and place at table will end up covered in food and he will not be pleasant to sit next to.

A major task of the speech therapist and the occupational therapist will be to encourage good feeding patterns, and they will have been working on this with the parents for some time before the child comes to school. At school, simple aids, such as adapted cutlery with curved polypropylene handles, will help children with minimal wrist and elbow movement (a full range of cutlery is available from Nottingham Rehab), or the handles of school cutlery can be enlarged by fixing on bike-handle grips, which are washable. If a child has the use of one hand only he could use a knife/fork combination (Nottingham Rehab), or adopt the American style of eating — cutting first with the knife and then transferring the fork into the functional hand and using it as a scoop. Plates can be stabilized with a Dycem mat (Nottingham Rehab), a gelatinous material that is non-slip on both sides, and there are clip-on clear plastic rims that act as a buffer to push food against when coordination is poor.

The child may feel that using aids to eat with 'shows him up' amongst his peers. This is a real fear and should be taken into consideration. Some children have been known to make great strides in their eating patterns when faced with this situation, but for those who are very poorly coordinated it has to be pointed out that a few aids which help them to eat without making a mess are more socially acceptable and will soon be ignored, whereas messy eating will not and cannot continue into adult life.

DIET

Motor impairment in itself does not indicate the need for a special diet. If the child is also a diabetic, then care must be taken to keep his glucose levels high and all staff should be prepared to allow him to eat a snack between lessons if necessary. He may also need additional carbohydrates — an extra potato on his dinner plate! Meals must be regular.

The greatest problem for children with physical limitations is that of overeating. Caring persons seem to feel that life as a disabled person must be so miserable that the only joy left to them is to eat. There is an element of truth in this and, of course, the children love being spoilt with sweets and sticky cakes. The reality, however, is that life as an obese person in a wheelchair is far worse, not only for the child but also for his parents and the care staff. Similar concerns apply to children of small stature.

Pain and fatigue

PAIN

The children most likely to be in pain as a result of a motor impairment are those with arthritis. Inflammation in the joints limits their freedom of movement and makes hand-work slow and painful. The combination of pain and frustration may make them tired and withdrawn and may lead to bad behaviour. At times when the condition is particularly painful, they will be helped in class by access to electrical aids such as typewriters, tape recorders and sewing machines.

Some children who have to spend all the time in a wheelchair are in danger of developing a curvature of the spine. It is quite probable that they will need to wear a splint that wraps around the upper half of their trunk. The splint is made of a rigid material and is closed at the front with Velcro straps. Not only is it difficult to take on and off but also, if it is positioned incorrectly, the child may experience pain under the arms or over the abdomen. Most children learn to live with this inconvenience but many suffer in silence rather than make a fuss. Care staff will need to be aware of possible discomfort and ensure that all is as it should be before the child returns to class after being changed.

Later in their school-days many of these children are then offered an operation to fix the spine by inserting a metal rod, so that the body splint need no longer be worn. After the operation and their return to school the position of the rod may alter and they will be in considerable pain whilst waiting for further treatment.

Most children who are wheelchair-mobile need to stand supported for some part of the day. This is to prevent or reduce 'contractures' at the hip and the knee. When the muscles around a joint become paralysed the joint will become stiff and 'locked' because of its lack of movement. If the joints are not moved regularly (preferably through their full range of movement every day), then the muscles will contract and get increasingly stiff. The physiotherapist will advise on exercises that can be done daily, either at home or in school by the care staff but, to reduce time out of class, they may suggest that the child stands in a frame (Figure 3.1) with work tray attached for some part of the day. Very often this causes the child pain; he will become distressed and it is extremely difficult for the teacher to stand by and watch, aware that this is best for him in the long term yet hating to see him suffer. It is best to take advice from the physiotherapist, who will be able to tell you just how much discomfort the child should bear. After all, most children can be great little actors and it might not be so bad after all!

Figure 3.1: A standing tray with work tray attached

Some children may be required to wear splints that either prevent deformities or allow a limb a degree of functional use. Children with a hemiplegia may wear a splint stretching from above the wrist to the joint between the fingers and the palm. This will prevent the wrist from 'dropping' and the fingers from curling into the palm of the hand. The child may be reluctant to wear the splint: it may hurt; it may make his arm feel hot and sticky; he may feel embarrassed — but he should be encouraged to do so because, by extending the wrist in this way, he may regain some functional use of his fingers. Try to grasp something with a limp wrist, you will find it almost impossible.

Noise can be pain to a child with a head injury. Whereas we take it for granted and instead notice silence, these children can be distressed by noisy classrooms or machinery in craft, design and technology classes. Sudden noise can trigger off a 'startle reflex' in children with cerebral palsy. The school electric bell may well cause him to throw up his hands and drop what he is doing, or knock things onto the floor. This factor has implications for his safety and that of the group.

FATIGUE

Children with a motor impairment, even those whose disability is minimal, will get more tired than the ordinary child. If movement patterns are affected because of neurological damage, then the child has to concentrate hard on controlling his limbs so that they will function normally. If we imagine what it would be like for us if we had to run all the time, than we can appreciate the amount of effort needed for a cerebral-palsied child to walk. The distances the child must travel during a school day need to be carefully considered, and for field trips alternative methods of transport may be necessary (taxi rather than public transport and a wheelchair provided upon arrival). Fatigue from general mobility difficulties will quickly be reflected in a deterioration of fine motor control and general lack of concentration.

Other children who will tire easily are those with muscular dystrophy. All the time the child is growing, the muscles that control movement are getting weaker. Once in a wheelchair the child may need arm supports attached to the chair so that he can concentrate all his efforts on maintaining hand function. Other children with limited hand function, such as those with arthritis, brittle bones and cerebral palsy, will all find writing and other forms of hand-work tiring and so provision needs to be made for this. Electric typewriters and computers will act as substitute pencils, but these children may still need to be provided with copies of maps, diagrams, graphs and so on, to save them time, effort and distress. In really difficult situations, the teacher or a classmate could provide copies of notes taken in class.

Finally, we all know what it is like to have a bad night, to wake after only a couple of hours sleep and have to face yet another day. Many children with motor impairment need to sleep in night splints; splints may need to be worn over any of the body's joints, and some wrap around the whole trunk. These are not comfortable, especially on a hot night, and the child may come to school very tired as a result. Children who have had recent head injuries may be experiencing difficulty returning to the normal patterns of sleep and wakefulness.

Teachers need to be aware that a tired child usually has a tired parent. As a consequence the child may arrive at school without breakfast or school books, dressed in a hurry and without due attention to hygiene. If this is the case, a half hour with the care staff, a cup of coffee and a biscuit, may be far more important for a successful day at school than attending assembly.

Medical needs

The additional needs of a child with motor impairment can quite easily be accommodated within the school's existing system for dealing with accident and illness. Most schools have a sick-bay, first-aid kit and regular visits from the school doctor. Some have a school nurse or member of staff who takes responsibility for minor problems.

Before a child with a motor impairment is admitted into a school the parents should supply a full list of possible medical and personal needs, along with emergency telephone numbers to include themselves or other responsible relative, the child's doctor and his hospital. The child's hospital registration number may prove to be extremely useful for speedy retrieval of case notes in an emergency.

DAMAGE

Some schools are very wary of accommodating a child with a physical difficulty. They are afraid that the child could fall and hurt himself more easily and do not want to take responsibility for this. Realistically one cannot guarantee that the child with special needs is not going to have an accident, any more than one can for any child. As long as normal care is taken to safeguard the whole school community, then the teachers will be doing all that they can in general terms.

However, there are certain conditions that lend themselves more easily to injury and an awareness of these is all that is necessary to allow a child with motor difficulties the usual freedoms. Such conditions are now considered in detail.

Fractures. Children with brittle bones are very prone to fractures; some more so than others. The condition usually improves as they get older but the teacher must realize that these children are just as likely to break a bone whilst turning over in bed as they are from being knocked into at school, and so teachers should not hold themselves responsible if an accident does happen.

Children with spina bifida or who are paraplegic as the result of an accident do run a greater risk of breaking bones. This is because the circulation in their legs is sluggish and the bones do not receive the necessary nourishment to maintain strong growth. They may be thin and brittle and may snap easily. Parents often think that exercise (walking in callipers) will damage their child, but the converse is true as improved circulation will strengthen muscles and bones. Because these children have no sensation they may not feel pain and so not know that they have damaged a limb. The first sign will be a firm, hard swelling. As the muscles are not strong there will be little pull on the fractured bone and it will not become too displaced. It may not be necessary to splint with a plaster cast and treatment will be limited to rest and not using callipers until the fracture has healed itself.

Children who are learning to walk on callipers, or who are generally unstable on their feet, may be encouraged to wear a padded skate-boarding or cycling helmet when they go outside. These can be purchased in attractive colours and are quite socially acceptable.

Diabetic children may bruise easily and so rough games in the playground or contact sports may be a problem.

Pressure sores. The biggest problem for a child with paraplegia, or who is mobile only by wearing callipers and walking with crutches, is the pressure sore. The paralysed parts of the body also have no feeling, and so it is impossible to know, apart from by looking, if a limb is pressing against a hard object (the side of a wheelchair, a poorly fitting calliper, the underside of a table, etcetera). This pressure will compress the skin, so preventing the circulation of oxygen, and as a result the skin tissue dies, producing an ulcer that may take weeks or even months to cure. A non-paralysed person moves continuously, even when seated, but the child in a wheelchair may not be able to redistribute his body weight so easily. He will need to be taught to take the weight on his arms and move his back whenever possible. If this can't be done he will need to sit on a special cushion to reduce the pressure.

Pressure sores are most likely to develop on areas of the body where the bones are closest to the surface of the flesh. The first sign will be a reddening of the skin, and if caught at this stage and pressure on the spot is relieved, all may be well. *If the skin is a bluish-black, then immediate medical attention should be sought.* Most paraplegic children are aware of this problem and are taught to examine themselves with the aid of a mirror on a flexible handle. They should do this every day whilst they are in bed or in the bath. Care staff should be aware of this problem and help the child to watch out for the positioning of their limbs, protruding objects tucked down inside a wheelchair, and any redness of the skin.

Burns and scalds. Again, because of a lack of sensation in the paralysed limbs, a child will not notice if he is sitting too close to a radiator or whether the cup of hot tea on his lap is burning his leg. He may not notice the heat of the sun. Sources of heat are a real hazard because the child has no natural reflex action that makes him move away fast. The problem is complicated by the fact that many children with motor impairment move clumsily or, if in a wheelchair, take up a lot of room. It is quite likely that this will cause them to brush against hot surfaces (an oven door or radiator) or knock into others carrying hot cups and dishes, the contents of which spill all over them. All children need to acquire their own survival code but the motor impaired child will need to be trained, and perhaps more than average attention will need to be paid to potentially dangerous objects within his environment.

DRUGS

The need for drugs has already been mentioned in relation to specific conditions. Most children take their drugs at home but should they need to take them whilst at school, either on a temporary or long-term basis, it is best to establish a routine that the child and the staff know about. Older children may prefer to take responsibility for this themselves, but this should only be allowed with the parent's permission.

When school outings or journeys are being planned that will stretch beyond the normal school day, it will be necessary to consult the parent and if necessary take the drugs with the first aid kit. The child may have to take them at regular intervals and a missed dose could have serious repercussions. Some epileptics need drugs immediately if a fit does not subside within a given space of time. If this is the case, and if the preparations are of the type that are inserted in the anus, the teacher will need to be taught how to administer them. Advice must be sought from the school medical officer with special reference to the legal implications of such action.

Inhalers for Asthmatics. Young children may need help to use their inhaler but older children should be able to manage this alone. There are various inhalers on the market but they all work in a similar way. If a school journey or outing is planned, then it will be very important to take the inhaler because a change in environment may trigger an attack, especially if the visit is to a farm (animals) in the countryside (pollen) and the cook has prepared a school picnic with 'treats' (allergies to certain foods).

Insulin injections. Usually these are a once-a-day occurrence and will be seen to by the parents or the child himself as he gets older. If a child is to take part in an extended school trip, then advice must be sought from the parents and supplies taken to cover the duration of the trip.

4 The Problems Posed by Limited Mobility

As student occupational therapists we were required to spend time with 'simulated disabilities'. Cooking supper with one hand tied behind the back might have seemed funny at the time but it certainly taught us what it must be like to have a paralysed arm. Without experiencing any degree of physical limitation to our otherwise healthy bodies it is difficult to put ourselves into the position of a child with a motor impairment. Ideally, when a school plans to admit a child with a physical difficulty, a member of staff, together with the child's potential peer group, should attempt to assume his particular problems and survey the school in advance of his arrival. Not only is this a practical and efficient way of eliminating many of the difficulties before the new pupil arrives, and of making his introduction to the mainstream less stressful, it is also one way in which the other children can be introduced to the idea of physical difficulty and special needs.

This chapter will look at the mobility problems that may be encountered by a child or young person with a motor impairment. Obviously, the degree of difficulty will relate to the degree of physical impairment but what we must remember is that our task is to minimize the mis-match between the child's needs and what the school environment is able to offer.

Getting to school and home again

Some children will be able to get to and from school independently, especially if they live nearby and can walk a short distance. However, the child who has a hemiplegia, or who needs to walk with sticks or crutches, will find long distances tiring and public transport at rush hour very frightening, especially when burdened down with school bags. If the child is in a wheelchair, then transport will have to be available. Most local authorities will provide a taxi and in some cases parents are willing to drive their child to school but having to rely upon hired transport can be an additional problem, especially when the taxi arrives late and will not collect at any other than a set time. The child's differences are highlighted when he is late for register, misses the first lesson and cannot stay for club (or a detention) after school. Flexibility needs to be built into any transport arrangements from the very beginning. (Further information from the Mobility Information Service and the Disabled Living Foundation for their Information Service Leaflet No. 8, *Transport*).

Access to school buildings

Full access to a building goes far beyond getting through the front door. The motor impaired child must have full access to all the facilities available to his peers. The Department of Education and Science (GB. DES, 1984a) publication, *Access for Disabled Students to Education Buildings* outlines the basic features of a school that need to be taken into consideration when planning full access arrangements for a child with mobility problems. These include entrances, maximum ramp gradients, width of doors and doorways, internal changes of level, adaptations to toilet facilities and appropriate means of escape.

One hopes that all new public buildings (including schools) are designed with access available to all, but today few new schools are being built and so one has to look at existing buildings with imagination and make the best of a difficult job.

Coping with steps

If a child has to wait for a ramp to be laid before he can get through the front door, then it is quite possible that he will miss a year or more of school whilst the wheels of bureaucracy turn. An occupational therapist will be able to measure up and advise on gradients, and possibly an enthusiastic PTA, after consultation with the Borough's Health and Safety Officer, will provide the funds and the expertise to construct them. Alternatively, portable ramps are available (information from the Disabled Living Foundation), which can be left in place only when required. Ramps are necessary for the wheelchair-mobile as well as for those who are wearing full-length callipers and using crutches. The less affected may be able to manage with extra handrails and half steps. Marking the edges of steps and other ground-level hazards with a contrasting paint is of general value but is especially useful for those children with a visual difficulty.

Coping with flights of stairs

Long flights of stairs present the greatest problem. Although it may be possible to accommodate a motor impaired child with his peer group at ground level in primary school, or for one or two years at secondary school, this eventually becomes too difficult. Not only does goodwill wear thin when it comes to the yearly problem of 'the timetable', but other children in other years may have similar difficulties and similar needs. Furthermore, one does not usually find the science labs, the home economics room, the art room and the gym all on the same floor! Sooner or later the problem has to be addressed, and it is more realistic economically and kinder to the pupil if such details are sorted out from the beginning.

If a lift is in existence already this is a bonus. But it may be so small that a child in a wheelchair would fill it and there would be no room for a helper. This could constitute a safety hazard, especially if the child could not turn his chair around inside or reach the buttons or the alarm bell. Stair lifts for wheelchairs are large and cumbersome and would take up too much room when a whole school is on the move, but a lift with a small seat (information from the Disabled Living Foundation) may be a suitable alternative for the child on crutches, or for the wheelchair child if a wheelchair is available on each floor and adult help is present to facilitate transfer.

The corridors are so long

Often the distances a child needs to travel between lessons are considerable. For the child who is a 'wobbly walker', or who needs to cope with sticks or crutches as well as carry books and possibly a typewriter, the corridors of a large secondary school at change-over time are more daunting than a large railway station in the rush hour. Partial use of a wheelchair for such journeys may be a safer alternative. Another option may be to let the motor impaired child leave the lesson five minutes early to give him a head start whilst the corridors are empty. An option possibly suited to a large school is the provision of two orthokinetic 'ponies' (Ortho-Kinetics (UK) Ltd.), one for outside and the ground floor and another for the first floor. The 'pony' is an attractive, electric buggy/bike — robust, easy to manoeuvre and easily fitting through most doorways. This system has been provided, for example, for a young lady who has spastic diplegia and walks with crutches; she could manage the stairs with adult help but the long distances on each floor and the open spaces of the playground were too much for her.

He has so much to carry

Walking up and down stairs and covering long distances is tiring but one also has to take into account the fact that the child needs to carry a school bag, sports gear and possibly a portable typewriter. Some children walk best with a rollator (described further on p. 60) to which can be attached a tray or a basket. The child in a wheelchair usually has a bag on the back or a tray in front but the child on sticks or crutches, or the 'wobbly walker', will have the most problems. We suggest that he wears a backpack with padded shoulders and that from an early age he learns to keep the day's work under subject headings in a hardback file. If at all possible, he should be allowed two sets of textbooks, one at home and one for his locker at school. This reduces the need to carry several exercise and textbooks, and work can be given in for marking in plastic folders and then stored at home in larger subject files. The child then has one hand free to hold onto the wall or the stair-rail and the other to hold his typewriter or games bag.

To relieve the pressure at social times such as play and meal breaks, kindly school secretaries or heads of year will often keep an eye on school bag and typewriter to avoid loss and to allow the child greater freedom of movement and social integration.

Access to classrooms and specific subject areas

Steps, stairs and long corridors present one set of problems; doors and doorways, room layout and furniture provide yet another. Again, the Department of Education and Science has published guidance (GB. DES, 1984b), which covers room layout for classrooms and for particular subjects and the specific design requirements for children with sensory difficulties. The bulletin was intended to be used as a basis for discussion between school, LEA and designer and would serve as a useful check-list in the planning stages.

Doors and doorways

Doors need to be wide enough to take the child's wheelchair; it may be that by removing a doorstop one can create that crucial extra inch or so in width. There also needs to be enough space both in front of and behind the door to allow him space to change direction if necessary. We have heard of a case where much money was spent on converting a toilet for disabled students, who arrived on their first day at college to discover that they could not even reach, let alone get through, the doorway! Additional hazards are rotating doors, doors on tight springs and doors with round handles. For children with poor balance and poor grip a lever handle may make all the difference; it may also be possible to remove the door-spring if it is not there for safety reasons (as on fire doors). Advice on a full range of door furniture that aids access for the disabled is available from specialist ironmongers (such as D.A. Thomas (London) Ltd.).

Classroom layout

A child in a wheelchair and a child on crutches or with a rollator will both need an equal amount of space to move around a room. At primary level, some children with crutches will abandon them and scoot around the floor on hands and knees, but this soon becomes socially unacceptable and does not improve overall mobility. They would be better encouraged to use the furniture as a prop as long as this does not upset the other children, which it might if they persist in falling against tables and knocking over paint pots and precious models!

At primary level it is easier to help the child by seating him in an area of the classroom close to the exit yet within easy reach of all the equipment he is likely to need — that is, paper, pencils, felt-tips, etcetera. Remember that a child in a wheelchair will not be able to reach as far as one who is upright. If he is using a typewriter that is mains-based, he will need to sit close to an electric socket, but it is to be hoped that soon most children at junior level and above will be using totally portable machines and, like secondary children at present, will be free to sit anywhere in the room.

At secondary level, it is almost impossible to create the ideal room layout. Children change rooms frequently and other groups may require the rooms to be set out in a variety of different ways. It should at least be possible to site a locker at a suitable height and if necessary enlarge the key handle to allow the pupil easy access.

Seating

Once classroom layout has been decided upon it is important to look more closely at where and how the child is to sit.

Unless the child is already well positioned in his own wheelchair, he should be given one that allows him to work at a table with his feet flat on the floor, his back well supported and his elbows at right angles to the table top. This is often difficult to achieve but it is important because even the child with the least motor impairment can easily become 'off balance' and this will affect his fine motor skills. Both table and chair heights can be adjusted by searching in other classrooms or the school-keeper's storeroom for alternative furniture, or by raising a table on blocks or providing a footrest for a higher chair (Figure 4.1). Again, flexibility and imagination are often the key to success. The wheelchair child may be able to work on his tray but this can isolate him from the group and it is best to try and match him to a table top around which other children are sitting.

It may be necessary to take into consideration the actual position of the child's chair within the room. This is important if the child has a visual

Figure 4.1: Blocks to raise the height of a table' the two heights 'x' are equal

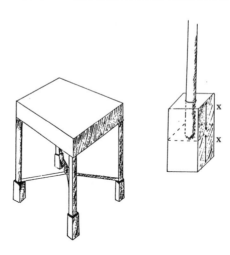

problem. He may prefer to be by a window so that more natural light falls on his work, but he may also need to be close to the chalkboard at an angle that allows the chalk to show up in good contrast against the black or green background. Correct lighting is very important for children with a visual difficulty. The type of lighting will vary according to the type of eye condition, and the needs of each individual child should be carefully considered.

Often we find that the motor impaired child, especially if he has additional learning problems, is placed at the front of the class alongside the 'naughty chair'. This does not do much for his confidence or self-esteem! At secondary level it is sometimes possible for the child with difficulties to hide away at the back of the classroom, causing no trouble but also not getting the attention that he so badly needs. General awareness and sensitivity on the part of the teacher is all that is really needed to position the child sensibly within the class group.

Adaptations to furniture in specific subject areas

Tables are of standard heights in primary and secondary classrooms and these heights may need to be adjusted to suit the individual child, but this becomes an impossible task when confronted by science benches, kitchen work-surfaces and art tables. These are matched to high stools for the able-bodied child but they are not accessible to the child in a wheelchair or one whose balance is not good enough to perch on an unstable stool. Ideas for getting round this difficulty may be had by visiting similar curriculum areas in a local special school for children with a physical disability, and with goodwill from the woodwork and metalwork departments it may be possible to adapt the tops of adjustable trolleys (Joncare, Oxford; F. Llewellyn and Co. Ltd., Liverpool) to hold cooker hobs or mobile science benches. The key points to consider are the adjustability of working-surface height, the distance that a child is able to reach from a seated position, ease of manipulating taps, knobs and switches, and the provision of stability for the equipment in use.

Toilet facilities

The motor impaired child who is incontinent needs privacy, as described in detail on p. 41. The school will need to provide a room with space for a wheelchair to turn around in, a bench that adjusts in height, wash basin, toilet and extractor fan. Ideally the toilet should have fitted rails and mirrors so that the child can be taught to be independent. There may be a need for a disposable bag unit. All the necessary fittings are available from specialist ironmongers (for example, D.A. Thomas (London) Ltd.).

Resources developed for one child with motor impairment will not inevitably become redundant. There will be other children who may or may not need similar provision on a long- or short-term basis at some point in their school life, possibly through temporary disablement. It is also to be hoped that the successful placement of one motor impaired child within the mainstream school will mean that more will be able to follow.

Aids to mobility

Shoes

For the child with poor coordination, shoes with laces are very difficult and, unless supportive boots are necessary, it is better if they can wear training shoes with Velcro fastenings (Velcro is readily available in haberdashery departments). Some children, however, have to wear surgical shoes. These are prescribed for them and are tight-fitting with long criss-cross laces. Few children can manage them without help. Sometimes children are loath to wear them because they look 'different', and their parents, in sympathy, don't make them do so. It is often the teacher's task to liaise between the physiotherapist and the parents when this happens — not an easy situation, but for the good of the child's mobility in the long term.

Sticks, crutches and rollators

Some children will be using one or two sticks or lightweight aluminium elbow crutches; care should be taken to ensure that their rubber ferrules do not become worn down so that they fail to grip the floor. These aids are also adjustable in height and will be set for each individual child by the physiotherapist. Wear and tear and inquisitive fingers may alter this setting — just another little thing to look out for! Rollators are walking frames that have two wheels at the front and two legs with rubber ferrules at the back. The child grips on to two handles over the wheels and pushes the aid along. They do provide greater stability in the early days of independent walking but are difficult to manage over uneven surfaces and take up a lot of space in a crowded classroom.

Callipers

Callipers are very different from the old fashioned leg-irons that we still see attached to little plaster figures 'begging' with attached collection boxes outside shops. Below-knee callipers are moulded plastic inserts that fit snugly around the heel and continue up the back of the calf muscle. They lend support to weak ankles and are easy to take off and replace for games and PE. Full-length callipers are made from lightweight metal and fit around the back of the hips with hinge joints at the hips and knees. Pins then fit the ends of the metal struts into holes on either side of the heels of the child's shoes. Children who need to use these, usually in conjunction with elbow crutches, will be able to explain to an adult how to take them on and off. Wearing underclothes and socks only, the child is usually lifted into them on a flat surface and they are fixed around his body with padded Velcro straps. When the child is raised to a standing position, care must be taken to see that the hinges are locked along the vertical axis. When sitting, the locks can be undone to allow flexion at hips and knees. The child's parents should be encouraged to provide him with loose-fitting trousers to go over the callipers (track suit bottoms are ideal) to make toileting and changing for games and PE so much easier. Callipers may rub and break down skin so creating pressure sores, which take a long time to heal. During this time, he cannot wear his callipers and so mobility is restricted. Those responsible for changing the child should look out for any problems of this nature and seek medical advice.

Prostheses/artificial limbs

These are usually provided for young children to encourage the development of muscle strength and the patterns of movement necessary to use these muscles effectively. An artificial arm is usually made of plastic or metal and has two 'fingers', covered in skin-coloured foam, which can grasp well enough to allow the child to hold a pencil, cut out, manage buttons and zips, and attend to his personal needs. If the child's shoulders are not very strong then a power-assisted arm may be provided. In both instances the child will be well supported by the occupational therapist, who will oversee his use of the aid.

As 'congenital amputees' usually have sensitivity in the remaining part of their limb, they may choose to use this rather than their prosthesis. They may also prefer to use their feet or their mouth to write with. If this is the case, then a revision of the child's seating and table height will be needed, but with imagination and flexibility, and with advice from the parents and therapist, this should not be a problem.

Children who have lost one or both lower limbs may be able to use artificial legs, but balance may be a problem and they will need to use crutches or a wheelchair. The balance of their trunk will be affected and this will mean that they take longer to be able to use a wheelchair efficiently.

Wheelchairs

These are provided by the Department of Health through the Artificial Limbs and Appliance Centres (ALACs) — in most large cities. They are prescribed by the child's family doctor or his consultant, and parents are provided with the names of firms who will provide maintenance. As the child's needs change and as he grows, he will need a chair for indoor as well as outdoor use; he may be prescribed a chair better suited to his postural needs and he will have to return to the wheelchair clinic for re-assessment. This can be a long drawn out process, which will affect decisions concerning his mobility around the school and may mean a change in the height of his working surfaces. Physiotherapists' hands are often tied and they cannot speed up this process. Patience will be necessary!

There are two types of wheelchair, manual and electric. If the child has good function in his trunk and upper limbs, he will be able to use a manual chair. The new lightweight chairs designed for sports look good and are easy to manipulate. If necessary, these can be pushed easily over difficult surfaces or lifted up and down stairs with the child remaining seated. They fold easily and fit into the boots of most cars. Battery-powered chairs offer increased mobility and therefore independence to those children who cannot operate a manual chair but they are much heavier and more difficult to transport. They also need to be charged overnight, and if the child does not take the chair home, this will have to be done by someone at school. Safe storage for this will need to be considered.

Manoeuvring a wheelchair requires more space than is sometimes realized. The child using it must take care to move with caution and not physically hurt his class-mates or cause damage to their work by bumping into tables. Some disabled children will persist in this behaviour. Possibly it is their only way of responding to personal anger and frustration, but this should not be tolerated. It has been known for particularly difficult youngsters to be immobilized when patience failed and the plug was pulled on their battery!

As a child grows older he should be taught to take responsibility for his own mobility and be able to tell others how to care for it and who to call for maintenance. A very good wheelchair proficiency course is run by the Royal Society for the Prevention of Accidents (ROSPA).

HINTS FOR WHEELCHAIR USERS AND HELPERS

Brakes. These should always be on when the child is getting in or out of the chair, whether helpers are with him or not. It is also useful to back a chair against a wall or other stable object during transfer.

Armrests. Often the arms of a chair are removable. Apart from allowing the chair to fold and pack flat for easy transport, this is to facilitate sideways transfer from wheelchair to chair, toilet seat or bed. To transfer easily the child will most likely use a board, along which he will 'bottom shuffle' from one location to the next. For this method to be effective it is useful for the adjacent surfaces to be of similar height. If armrests are detachable, take care not to lift the chair by its arms only as these will fall off, the child may fall out or you may get a crushed toe!

Footrests. Never let the user or any other child stand on the footrests. When the user starts to get out of his chair ensure that these rests are taken off or swung to the sides. Most chairs will tip forwards if the footrests are stood upon.

Kerbs; uneven ground. Even a child who can propel his own chair may need a little help. When a chair is pushed *down* over an obstacle the tipping lever beside the back wheels should be operated by the helper so that the chair tips backwards. As the larger rear wheels go down over the obstacle, the weight will be taken by the helper. Take care to hold both handles and distribute the weight evenly. Once the rear wheels are down the front can be lowered and the chair can go forward. To push a chair *up and over* an obstacle is more difficult. The chair is tipped once again by using the tipping lever beside the rear wheels; the small front wheels will then ride up onto the kerb. The rear of the chair then needs to be lifted. If the kerb is high or the child is heavy, then two helpers may be needed, one to lift the chair from the front wheels (not the footrests).

Speed. Do not allow the child's class-mates to push the chair too quickly. This will be difficult to ensure but rules should be made from the beginning. All children love games but the immobile child can be frightened if his chair is bumped, jerked, started or stopped too quickly. Whereas a child in a pram is usually seated facing his pusher and can anticipate changes in direction or in speed, the child in a wheelchair will be facing ahead. Speed can be very frightening if the brick wall at the end of the playground looms dangerously near, a road has to be crossed or a busy pedestrian precinct has to be negotiated.

Lifting for transfer. If a child needs to be lifted regularly, for transfer or for toileting, then the helper and class teacher should take instruction from the physiotherapist, the occupational therapist, or the parents who, after all, do this all the time. It is very easy to do permanent damage to the back through incorrect balance whilst lifting weights.

Mobility at playtime

Many children with motor impairment get a great deal of fun and necessary exercise by riding a bicycle. It is, after all, a 'normal' mobility aid. They may have problems with balance so it may have to be a tricycle. If they cannot use their feet in the conventional way, it will be necessary to use a modified version or adapt the pedals. Tricycles are accepted as mobility aids by the Department of Health and should be available to children over five years old.

The 'Tri-Aid', for example (Tri-Aid Manufacturing Ltd., East Kilbride), a hand-propelled tricycle, is popular with most primary age children. It has safety brakes and is hand-operated. A range of footrests is available and it is large enough to be ridden with full-length callipers. This is an important point because most tricycles cannot be ridden unless the knee is bent. Storage may be a problem in the mainstream school but the nature of the aid will enable the child more natural integration during one of the most difficult times of all, playtime.

Safety factors

Teachers often raise the issue of safety, both of the child and of the school community as a whole, when the integration of a motor impaired child is being considered. They are worried that they will be held responsible if there is an accident. Many consider that the child will be more vulnerable as a result of his medical condition or limited mobility.

Staff have to be realistic and accept that if an accident is going to happen, it is just as likely to be the more mobile able-bodied child who is involved as it is the one with the impairment. It may comfort teachers to know that legally they are expected to exercise a standard of care equal to that of a reasonably careful parent. Neither the headteacher nor any other has automatic legal liability for any injury to the child whilst he is in their care. In order to establish liability, negligence or carelessness on the part of the teacher as the direct cause of the accident must be proved.

Before the child starts school it would be wise to talk to his parents; their experience of possible danger areas will be invaluable. They will feel relieved that the teacher is planning with such care and the teacher will be forewarned of their attitudes and expectations. Although some parents may be over-protective, many want their child to have the same experiences as his peers and are willing to risk the odd bumps and bruises.

The teacher should also know exactly what to do in case there is an accident or the child is taken ill. She should have to hand the various emergency telephone numbers (see p. 50), the child's hospital registration number and the name of his consultant. This information should be readily available to all staff in case the class teacher is absent; it should accompany the child on any school outing. The headteacher should check that the child is covered by the school insurance policy if he is to go with his class on a school journey. The charges for a child with a physical disability are higher than usual.

Vulnerable children will be those with poor coordination, those who walk slowly or who have difficulty balancing. If the child is in a wheelchair, accidents usually occur when someone else is in charge, but such a child is likely to be prone to bruising and fractures because of limited sensation and circulation in the paralysed limbs. The child who has epilepsy, or whose sight and hearing is defective, will also be at risk. Having said this, it would appear that every child with a motor impairment needs to be carefully watched in case he comes to some harm!

The teacher must assess the safety needs of each child and respond appropriately. Once a list of precautions has been decided upon, this should be circulated amongst the other staff, and all welfare assistants should have a copy as it is they who will be supervising the child outdoors during play.

Like all public buildings, schools are subject to fire regulations. There may be little problem if it is a one-storey building, but where there are two or more floors the child who is in a wheelchair or slow to walk on crutches may, at first sight, present problems for those who are responsible for the enforcement of those regulations. With a little imagination it is usually possible to find a way in which to satisfy the authorities. However, emergency evacuation plans should be discussed in school with the health and safety officer and the child's parents.

When travelling by car or bus in a wheelchair, the child must be strapped into the chair and the chair strapped to the vehicle. To check that school transport conforms to the standards set down by the Department of Transport, contact their Disability Unit for their training video, which is available on free loan to anyone who carries disabled passengers, and also for their Code of Practice.

5 Educational Implications of Motor Impairment
1. Practical Issues

Defining the problem

As we have seen, to have a motor impairment means that one cannot, for one reason or another, control the movements of the body to perform certain tasks in a normal way. A child may not be able to walk without staggering; he may not be able to coordinate his knife and fork in order to eat without making a mess.

The reasons for these difficulties will be neurological in origin (Chapter 3) and the degree of impairment will depend upon the degree of damage to the central nervous system. For this reason, when looking at motor impairment and its effect upon the child's ability to play a full part in the school curriculum, it is convenient to separate disorders of movement that are purely *motor* in origin from those that are the result of a *perceptual–motor deficit*.

Motor disorder

If a child has to use a wheelchair, crutches or sticks or walks in a very unsteady way, it is going to be obvious both to himself and his teachers what activities he will and will not be capable of. Team sports and certain elements in PE will prove to be difficult or will need to be modified to include him. This does not mean to say that sport is a 'no-go area'. A growing number of disabled athletes are proving to the world just how many activities they are capable of undertaking. As has already been discussed, attention will need to be paid to overall access to buildings and classrooms to allow integration into a full curriculum.

Unfortunately, unless the impairment only affects the lower limbs (as in spinal injury), there is usually some involvement of the upper limbs and hands. The child with muscular dystrophy whose muscles grow gradually weaker will find it more and more difficult to grip a pencil and press hard enough to make a mark on the paper. The child with cerebral palsy will have increased muscle tone in hand and arm and any attempt at controlled movement, such as writing, will be difficult if not impossible. Some children have a tremor in the upper limb. As soon as they start upon a hand-skill activity their hand begins to shake uncontrollably (intention tremor; Chapter 3).

Motor difficulties of this nature can be helped by the provision of aids such as typewriters with guards fitted over the keyboard, spring loaded scissors, Dycem matting (p. 46) and specially designed gadgets to help independence in the home economics room, science laboratories and technical workshops. These will be dealt with later in this chapter.

Perceptual–motor difficulties

It has become increasingly accepted that difficulties in visual perception and problems in coordination and movement can all affect classroom learning. It is accepted that the two defects are associated. Skilled motor behaviour is essential in many aspects of day-to-day living; through movement we interact with our physical and social environment. We often take the ability to make purposive movements for granted. Because we are so used to getting dressed, handling cutlery, opening the post, locking the front door and so on, we don't take time to think about the complex processes underlying the performance of simple and habitual tasks. We only consider the acquisition of a specific skill to be an achievement when it is a totally new one such as driving a car. Then we may stop and think about the fact that all motor skills that are already familiar or are being practised demand a balanced interaction between many physiological and psychological processes.

Immaturity of movement can be illustrated by watching a child handle tools such as a rule or a hammer. Possibly, when he is washing you will notice that he wrings the sponge or the flannel out with one hand, being unable to bring both hands into the mid-line and rotate them in opposite directions. The action will be similar to that of a four-year-old, simple and ineffective. The child will need specific practice in order to develop skills we take for granted.

The terms *agnosia* and *apraxia* are usually used to describe the loss of well-developed function (some adults have this as the result of a stroke). Today they are sometimes also used to describe an interference with the development of these functions. Thus when they are applied to children we may see on a child's notes that he has 'developmental agnosia' or 'developmental apraxia'.

Put simply, agnosia is the inability to interpret sensory information. Normally sensation and perception are two aspects of a single process; perception is sensation reinforced by memories and images derived from past experiences and called up by association. If the association areas in the brain are damaged, then there will be difficulty in planning and carrying out a connected series of movements. Apraxia is an inability to carry out purposive movements, for even though there is adequate physical ability for their performance, the organization is lacking. Defects of perception and motor organization are the two main difficulties with which the 'clumsy' child has to cope. He may show a predominance of one or the other but most children who fall into this category show a marked involvement of both functions and both fine and gross movements are affected.

You may read on the therapist's report that he has very poor kinaesthetic sense. *Kinaesthesis* is the sense that tells you what position your body is in and where your limbs are. If you are asked to close your eyes and hold both hands out in front of you with one higher than the other, you should be able to identify which hand is higher and which lower. The child with a perceptual–motor difficulty who is also dyskinaesthetic will not be able to do this. Most people can write their name with their eyes closed, but for him, again, this will be extremely difficult. The child will have to struggle to control the movement necessary to make a single letter with his eyes wide open, Kinaesthesis is an important sense because it allows us to detect errors of movement and so correct them. It tells us when we have moved too fast, when we have over-reached, when we are about to fall off a chair — errors are sensed kinaesthetically. We do not remember the muscles we have moved but we remember the movement; this is stored and the movement improved upon. We have the ability to learn the right action for the task. The child with poor kinaesthetic sense does not have this ability. Each attempt to catch or kick a ball, or to copy letters, is as if it was the first.

Often we do not know a child has a perceptual–motor difficulty until he is required to learn how to write. There is no clinical picture of the child who some may describe as 'clumsy' but the parents may be able to describe a history of delayed development. Compared with older siblings or peers at the nursery, the child may have been later to sit up, stand for the first time and walk. Once up and moving he was prone to falls and ran awkwardly. He would have been slow to learn how to dress himself and it is most likely still quicker for his mother to get him ready for school. Once at school, poor fine and gross motor skills will both affect his overall performance. He will not be good at sport and will be the last to be chosen for a team. His writing will be untidy and he may reverse letters, numbers or whole words; spelling will prove difficult.

Unfortunately, perceptual difficulties do not go away easily, however bright the child. If the brain does not interpret what is seen accurately, then decisions will be made on the wrong information. Not only will the ability of the child (or adult) be underestimated but he may also be at risk in certain situations. A strange or crowded setting may disorientate and confuse him. Crossing busy roads or coping with unfamiliar surroundings will be difficult, driving a car safely may prove impossible, and working with machinery in a factory could be positively dangerous.

Successful motor development is essential if a child is to explore his environment and learn through experience. Later he will be able to express the ideas and concepts so learned through drawing and writing. The ability to move efficiently is also necessary for social and emotional development, which grows naturally through the freedom to interact with others in play and to communicate through gesture and speech. The child who is able to move with ease and perform motor tasks skilfully will be growing in self-confidence and building a positive self-image. It has been argued that the child who cannot control his movements adequately develops a poor self-concept and encounters difficulties in social and emotional adjustments. .

The effect of motor impairment on a child's self-concept will depend greatly upon how the child's performance both at home and at school is viewed by the important adults in his life, by his peers and by himself. It is counterproductive to insist that a child should complete activities that will lead to failure. It is better to try and develop self-confidence through activities where he will be successful. Once self-confidence is established, he will be more ready to experiment with and practise those skills that he finds difficult without threat to his self-concept.

Assessing the degree of difficulty

The child who is diagnosed as having cerebral palsy or spina bifida will have annual assessments, and the nature of his school placement will be determined by his ability to manage both physically and academically. Issues such as extra teacher support, therapy and the need for care staff should have been sorted out before he arrives. The fact that any learning difficulties are likely to be the result of his particular 'condition' will be recognized, and the teacher can start immediately to assess his strengths and weaknesses, either by way of her own teaching experience or through standardized tests.

However, many children who have perceptual–motor difficulties are not diagnosed at an early age and their difficulties may not be apparent until they are faced with the personal independence expected of them at school. Because a child is slow and messy, many a parent will continue to dress and feed him in order to save time; this further complicates the problems as the child has no time to practise the skills he finds difficult. In addition, the complex tasks of learning to read and write prove too much and the child will avoid these activities if he can. Once the teacher notices that a child is not matching up to his peers and stops to ask why, she may find that the parents have been asking the same question for years but have not been able to get any satisfactory answer. They will have noticed (or friends and relatives will have told them!) that this child did not match up to his siblings or peers when it came to physical skill and personal independence. They may have had him referred to an orthopaedic specialist because of poor balance and frequent falls when a paediatric neurologist would have been more appropriate. Their doctor may have put it all down to a 'maturational lag' and told them that he would 'grow out of it'.

Thankfully, behaviour that until recently would have given the medical profession, educational psychologists, teachers and possibly parents cause to suspect that a child was mentally retarded or behaviourally disturbed is now more likely to be seen to be the result of a degree of neurological impairment. This manifests itself in a significant delay in motor development, plus a degree of incoordination unacceptable for the child's age on developmental checks. As a result of the 1981 Education Act (GB. DES, 1981) a full assessment of special educational needs requires both a multiprofessional and parental contribution so that all the child's strengths and weakness can be recorded and considered before appropriate support and remediation is provided.

To describe the many forms of neurological and psychological assessment currently in use in health clinics and schools is beyond the scope of this book. However, it is important for the mainstream teacher to be familiar with the most commonly used tests and to be able to interpret them in relation to planning remedial activities for the child.

Pre-school developmental screening

The routine developmental screening tests carried out in health clinics during the first 18 months of life will detect severe subnormality or cerebral palsy but not minimal motor impairment if this is slight or highly specific. Later birthday checks and pre-school checks are far more likely to identify poor gross and fine motor coordination, and research does show them to be valuable as predictors of later difficulty.

There is no shortage of appropriate tests for very young children; Bate *et al.*, (1981) review 49 of them. However, nursery teachers would argue that formal tests are never subtle enough to capture the mix of abilities, attitudes and social skills which the close observation of children during everyday play can provide. From play the teacher should be able to judge concentration span, hand preference and strength, visual perceptual skills (shape matching by trial and error, or by deduction), conceptual and language development. Tests may provide a scientific assessment of a child's abilities but they are stressful and therefore possibly inaccurate. In an 'integrated' nursery it will be easy to identify the child with problems and, by matching him against the 'norm', make realistic judgements of his performance levels.

In constructing the *Sheridan Stycar* charts (Sheridan, 1973) of children's developmental progress, Mary Sheridan, like others in Europe and America, drew upon the work of Arnold Gesell, who was both a child psychologist and a paediatrician. Sheridan's intention was to design a much-needed paediatric tool. The purpose of the charts is to monitor the developmental progress — the 'stepping stones' of normal children — and in so doing learn how to detect the earliest signs of physical disability, mental handicap, personality disorder or social difficulty. The charts are well illustrated and are easy to understand. They do not produce a 'quotient' of any sort.

School-entry screening

The best time for this screening is during the first year at school when the class teacher can discuss specific difficulties with the school medical officer and the parents.

There are many 'checklists' available to the teacher; some education authorities publish their own. The *Croydon checklist*, for example, was designed by Sheila Wolfendale as an awareness-raising tool for teachers to use with children at the end of their first term in school (Wolfendale, 1976). The test covers four main areas, speech and language, perceptual–motor, emotional-social and the general response to learning situations. Of special relevance to the child who may prove to be motor impaired is a booklet extracted from the main theme of that work, entitled *Handbook for Teachers, Perceptual Motor Training* (Wolfendale and Bryans, 1987), which outlines an observation sheet and then gives advice on how to design a perceptual–motor programme. Ideas for training specific deficits are given in the text. The strength of this approach is that the chosen activities are those all children enjoy and so the child with difficulties can be helped in a group context.

The *Aston Index* (Newton and Thomson, 1982) is also designed for teachers to use in the classroom. It consists of 17 sub-tests, of which nine have been standardized for children between 5 and 14 years of age. For a further three items the handbook gives guidance on abilities expected at certain age levels; the remaining five are dependent upon the tester's judgement. The test is divided into two levels: level 1 is for children who have been at school for about six months and examines pre-reading skills; level 2 is for children from seven years and older whose basic skills relating to reading, writing and spelling are causing concern. The results of each sub-test are recorded on the score sheets and then plotted on two profile sheets — one to illustrate the child's general ability and attainment, thereby giving an indication of mental age; the other to record specific performance items indicating those skills the child will need to acquire written language. As the normative profiles for three age levels are given for the performance items, it is possible to interpret the child's perceptual ability.

The *Aston Index* has a follow-on *Aston Portfolio*, which includes useful teaching ideas in response to specific areas of weakness. The test takes about an hour to administer in a one-to-one setting, and a second hour to calculate the results. As such, it is time-consuming but the results are useful to the teacher. The teacher and child will need access to a room with space for some movement, a table and chair for the child, and a chair for the teacher with small table to set out the test materials.

The *Test of Motor Impairment* (Henderson revision; TOMI; Stott *et al.*, 1984) can be administered by educational psychologists, therapists and teachers. The structure of the test gathers information that measures motor impairment in children from five years of age upwards. Norm-based scores indicate average, borderline or failed performance compared with the child's, peers; above average ability is not recorded. The tester is required to observe those aspects of motor difficulty, motivation and emotional response that may contribute to failure. Items in the test have been devised to assess ability in manual dexterity, ball skill and balance. The tests are graded in difficulty and divided into four age bands, 5–6 years, 7–8 years, 9–10 years and over 11 years. The interpretation of the results is based on norm-based scores that provide a motor impairment score of between 0 and 16, plus the test's observations, which highlight significant motor deficits or faults in coping style. The child who scores 6+ shows a definite degree of motor impairment but the need for remediation will depend upon whether re-testing at a lower age level shows a high degree of motor impairment or a generalized motor delay. *TOMI* does not include guidelines for remediation but can be used again to measure progress.

TOMI is an expensive test and so not likely to be readily available in an individual school. We are finding that occupational therapists are becoming skilled in its administration (see Chapter 2). Children are tested on a one-to-one basis; it takes about an hour with a second hour for scoring and interpreting the results. The therapist and child need access to a room about 18 by 12 feet (6 by 4 metres), with one blank wall.

Psychological tests

Children are usually referred to the educational psychologist because of learning difficulties or behavioural problems. If learning difficulties go unnoticed, then behaviour problems often occur. The child may just give up, become apathetic and withdraw; he will quite possibly be a lonely child with few friends. It is more face-saving to lean on the playground fence, out of the way of the ball, pretending lack of interest in something that you can't catch than to admit that you cannot join in the fun. Who wants a clumsy child on their team? Sometimes the child will still give up trying but cover this by becoming the class clown, redirecting the teacher's attention from his work to his behaviour, which quite possibly gives him a certain status in the class that he can hide his difficulties behind. Some children can become frustrated and will develop aggressive behaviour. Psychosomatic aches and pains are often used so that the child does not have to expose himself to situations where he needs to have physical skills. Observations may show that the child complains of pains in the joints or perhaps vomits just before art, CDT, PE or games. Sometimes they just don't want to come to school.

Until the development of the *Stott Test of Motor Impairment* (1972) and the more recent *Henderson Revision TOMI* (p. 71), the most useful test had been Lauretta Bender's *Visual Motor Gestalt Test* (Bender, 1938), which is sensitive enough to pick out children with very fine motor coordination difficulties. The optimum age to administer this test is eight years old. The test consists of nine cards, each bearing a line drawing originally used by Wertheimer in his experimental work on visual perception. Each card is presented to the child, who copies it onto a plain sheet of paper working at his own speed; these reproductions are then scored. The power of the test is not in the final score obtained but in the observation and analysis of the way in which he goes about the task, how he grips his pencil, where he starts to draw on the page, etc.

The *Wechsler Intelligence Scale for Children* (WISC; Wechsler, 1949) is used frequently. Without knowing something about the child's overall ability it is impossible to interpret the results of motor coordination tests. One child may be clumsy and mentally handicapped, another may be clumsy and of well above average intelligence. The *WISC* is valuable for the assessment of children aged from 7 to 16 years because it allows a comparison between the verbal and the non-verbal ability of the child. Children with a motor impairment very often show discrepancies between their verbal and performance IQs. The value of the assessment is that it will tell the teacher if the child is potentially able and, if this is the case, then she will need to look further in searching for the reasons for his difficulties.

Psychological assessments may have a therapeutic value in that the psychologist can feed back information about the child's abilities and disabilities in a positive and constructive way to both parent and child. When behaviours that have been causing stress can be accounted for, everyone concerned feels that they can make a new start. However, knowing the child's general ability level or being able to pin-point those areas where he is functioning below the expectations of his chronological age is worthless unless the results can be communicated to the teacher and, through discussion practical teaching ideas, can be found to help overcome his weaknesses.

Handwriting difficulties

Functional use of the hands is important in fulfilling long-term educational goals. It is very rare that a child with a motor impairment does not have some difficulty with fine motor skills. Even if the disability is not obviously physical, it may be motor–perceptual in origin. In order to be able to access a mainstream curriculum it is expected that the child will be able to write.

Efficient handwriting is necessary for all school work; those children who cannot or do not achieve this skill are at an immediate disadvantage. Being unable to write, for whatever reason, deprives a child of one method of communication. In our society, being unable to communicate through the written word hinders access to the school curriculum, the examination system and eventually to many forms of employment and adult independence.

If the child has a marked impairment affecting all hand activity (such as increased muscle tone in the hand, tremor or paralysis), then it is better to consider the provision of alternative means of recording, such as an electronic typewriter. If the impairment is not obvious, a first response is to try to improve his handwriting through a full assessment and specific teaching. We may be moving towards the time when children will be carrying around pocket computers with keyboards as they now do calculators but, for the foreseeable future, they will still need to fill in forms and sign their name without resorting to an electronic aid.

By matching a short explanation of the individual skills needed if a child is to achieve efficient, fluent handwriting with the difficulties known to result from some degree of motor or perceptual–motor impairment, will help the teacher to understand how damage to the central nervous system, however minimal, could affect the ability to write. This comparison is made in Table 5.1

Table 5.1: Matching handwriting skills with the effects of impairment

Skill necessary	Impairment
To see accurately	Poor eyesight/squint
To be able to make sense of the model to copy and of what to do in order to guide and control hand and arm movements	Difficulty in organizing feedback from various senses, that is, cannot pick out figure from background or find the odd one out
	Visual and kinaesthetic feedback processes are delayed
To control muscles of hand and arm	1. Damage to the cerebellum, which controls voluntary movement, and to motor cortex, which affects upper limb functioning
	2. Shoulder girdle instability limits the child's ability to control hand movement — he may prefer to change dominance to the non-preferred hand if that shoulder is more stable
	3. Has had to use hands to support body rather then develop fine motor skills
To order his movements correctly; that is, copy pattern (also do up buttons, thread beads)	Cannot organize movements in space; slow to develop hand preference
Concentration and motivation	Limited concentration span; awareness of failure leads to reluctance to try

However, not all children will have this degree of disability yet still be unable to write legibly and at speed. Assessment may identify some practical issues which may be the cause of his difficulty.

Seating

Balance may be a problem and, if this is so, a seat so high that the child's feet swing off the floor will disturb his posture and make hand control more difficult. Ensure that the child sits with his feet flat on the floor, his back supported and his forearms resting comfortably on the writing surface. This may mean raising the height of the table or providing a foot block. A sheet of Dycem matting (p. 46), cut to fit the seat of the chair, will anchor a wriggling bottom! Research has shown that a slopping writing surface, such as the Write Angle desk-top writing aid (Phillip and Tacey, Andover), can have a positive effect upon poor handwriting. It may even help to control hand tremor.

Seating position within the classroom

If the child is expected to copy from the board, then he must have a clear view of it and sit facing it. The child with perceptual problems will find it difficult to transfer his attention from a vertical surface to a horizontal one, to remember his place on both, and to retain a visual image of the work to be copied. If he also has to turn his body, then we are asking the impossible. If it can be arranged, light should fall on the writing page so that the body or the writing hand do not cast a shadow.

Hand preference and paper position

Many children are late to develop a dominant hand and are allowed to decide in their own time with no disastrous results. The child with a motor difficulty will need to develop strength and flexibility in the preferred hand and so consistency for one side should be encouraged as soon as is practicable. The *Aston Index* (p. 71) includes a 'laterality' test, or the teacher can check handedness as follows:

1. Sit directly opposite the child across the table.
2. Ask the child to place both hands on the table in the mid-line (in front of his body).
3. Place a pencil in the centre of the table and ask the child to pick it up and write.
4. Observe which hand he picks up with and which he writes with.
5. Repeat the exercise several times to identify the dominant hand.
6. To remind the child to use his dominant hand it may be necessary to provide him with a writing board marked with a pencil on one side and an outline of the hand he uses to stabilize his paper on the other (Stollard, 1988).

If a child seems very delayed in the development of a preferred side, it is difficult to advise on which hand should be encouraged. Observation of competence in a variety of tasks may identify the more dominant hand. The occupational therapist should be able to advise and provide ideas for activities to encourage hand function and laterality.

If a right-handed child has to sit next to a left-hander at the same table, the right-hander should sit to the right-hand side so that elbows do not get in the way.

Take care that the piece of paper is not too large; a child with short stature or with small limbs due to brittle bones will not have a very long reach. Correct paper position is also essential (Figure 5.1), especially for the left-hander, who will need to see what he has written. Dycem matting (p. 46) will hold paper in position but, if the child has a regular place in class, it may be possible to mark the correct paper position with masking tape stuck to the table.

Figure 5.1: Position of paper for (a) left—and (b) right-handers

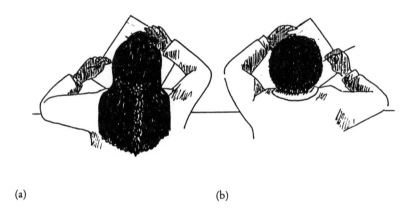

(a)   (b)

Pencil grip

Handwriting experts maintain that the most effective pencil grip is the 'tripod grip'. It is usually less tense for the hand and arm muscles and it is a grip that allows speed without muscle fatigue. Many nursery and infant classes attempt to encourage this grip by offering thick-shafted pencils but these are often too long and heavy for the child with weak grip or poor motor skills. It is better to enlarge the shaft of the pencil with a piece of Plasterzote or sponge-rubber tubing (Nottingham Rehab) attached with masking tape; this is light and soft to the touch. Children can be helped by using triangular pencils or triangular plastic sleeves that slip onto regular pencils. LDA (Cambridge) supply a wide range of writing aids, and recently have added Stetro moulded pencil grips to their range. For the older child, an elastic band wrapped round the pencil or pen at about 1 inch (2.5 cm) up the barrel will reduce a tense grip and prevent the fingers from slipping down to the writing point and obscuring their writing. Allow the child to try out a wide range of pens and pencils. Some children prefer to use a felt-tip pen, which provides a certain stability as it moves across the paper.

Pressure on the paper

If a child is very small (small stature/brittle bones) his sitting position will not allow the kinaesiological pressure from the whole body to be trans-mitted through the arm to the hand so that it can make a strong mark on the paper. The child with muscular dystrophy will have diminishing power for both grip and pressure on a writing implement and may write better with felt-tip pens. Some children tend to press too hard, so restricting the flow of the pencil across the paper. This is usually the result of faulty grip or the wrong writing tool, but either way it makes writing difficult to read and hin-ders fluency. The degree of pressure can be adjusted by experimenting with sheets of writing paper and carbon paper; the ideal pressure makes a fair copy with two sheets of paper and one carbon in between. Children enjoy this activity, and it teaches them to 'feel' and control their muscle tone, a skill that could generalize to other activities requiring fine motor coordina-tion.

Writing at reasonable speed

Some children with a minimal degree of impairment are able to develop a reasonable hand that is efficient during their primary school years. At sec-ondary school, when there is pressure upon them to write at speed and to copy from the board, a book, or take notes for consideration periods of time, the skill breaks down. The child with motor–perceptual difficulty will find that looking away from his writing back to the text and so on will dis-turb the rhythmic flow. Some children will not have the muscle strength or coordination to cope, or it may be that their handwriting style is faulty.

A good basic assessment tool is the *Handwriting File* (Alston and Taylor, 1985). The check-list not only covers the practical aspects of handwriting, such as pencil grip and letter formation, but also whether children know their letter names and sounds; it then goes on to suggest ways in which faulty technique can be corrected. To determine whether a secondary-school age child is writing as speedily as his peers is more difficult. When assessing this, you may like to use the following test and match the result against the following norms.

The test. Ask the child to write a familiar sentence such as '*The quick brown fox jumps over the lazy dog*' over and over again for three to five minutes.

Norms for handwriting speed suggest that:

A child of	7 years writes	28 letters a minute
	8	36
	9	45
	10	52
	11	60
	12	67
	13	75 or 13–15 words
	16	20 words a minute

If handwriting becomes illegible and the child distressed when under such pressure, then an alternative method of recording work should be considered.

Which paper?

Mainstream infant classrooms prefer the children to use unlined paper so that they can explore and practise pre-writing and pattern skills, concentrating only on correct formation. Later, when letter shapes are more formally introduced either as letters or as more complex patterns, some teachers prefer to use paper with single lines well spaced, or double tramlines, so that the child can see which letters fit on and between the lines and which continue above and below it. Children with spina bifida and hydrocephalus benefit greatly from using lines. Otherwise their handwriting may start at the top left-hand corner of the page but, by the end of a sentence, they will be well on the way to the bottom right!

Print or cursive?

When children are taught to write they usually learn how to print, the 'ball and stick' approach. This means that when they move on to 'joined up' writing they have to learn to write all over again. In our experience, many youngsters with handwriting difficulties who fail at secondary level do so because they are trying to 'join up' printed letters. Christopher Jarman (1982) suggests the basic modern hand, which introduces linking movements from the start. This teaches the child to start and finish the letter in the correct place so that the letters will join naturally, one to the other. When letters are joined up in plain 'cursive' script, words are seen as *visual gestalts* and the spaces fall automatically between the words. Individual letters that use the same movement patterns can be taught in 'families', with those that are easily reversed taught in different groups and rarely confused.

Remedial activities

The fine motor skills of a child with spina bifida can be helped greatly if, from a very early age (Rosenbaum *et al.*, 1975), they are encouraged to work on improving them. This would suggest that any child with minimal cerebral dysfunction/motor impairment will benefit in a similar way. The following are some ways of responding to handwriting difficulties but the list is not exhaustive and the teacher should refer to the work of Jarman (1982), and of Alston and Taylor (1985; 1987) and Hancock and Alston (1986), for a more comprehensive approach. Obviously the activities should be matched to the needs and the age level/self-image of the child.

TO DEVELOP MUSCLES AND EXPERIENCE THE SHAPE OF LETTERS IN OTHER WAYS

1. Make letter shapes in plasticine, clay or pastry dough.
2. Trace letters in finger paint or sand trays.
3. Cut letter shapes from different materials; the child finger traces over these to develop his tactile memory.
4. Trace letter shape on child's back or the palm of his hand; play recognition games with or without a visual prompt.

TO DEVELOP THE 'FEEL' OF MAKING LETTERS

1. Use chalk on chalkboard, or large paintbrushes at an easel. Progress from a vertical to horizontal plane.
2. Use Osmiroid 'Roll 'n Write' plastic letters (LDA, Wisbech) to help the child observe how letters are formed.

3. Practise tracing letter shapes from a model placed under clear acetate (Clearview Write Away; Philip and Tacey, Andover) so that mistakes can be easily wiped away.
4. Encourage child to state name and sound of letter and then 'talk' his way through drawing it; for example, d = 'around, right up and down'. Many children confuse letters that sound alike (t, d, c, g, p, b) or letters that look alike (n, h, r). The small changes in position of mouth and tongue and throat when voicing the vowel sounds are difficult to recognize. Learning to write letters correctly whilst naming them will help the child with perceptual motor difficulty to make these discriminations and associations. Discrimination between letter names is easier than between the sounds.
5. Encourage tracing activities — these eliminate any need to make spatial judgements about direction and distance as is necessary when copying from a model (develops kinaesthetic memory).
6. Use an overhead projector to trace over patterns, letters and words, looking only at the screen (develops kinaesthetic memory).
7. Write letters with eyes closed (develops kinaesthetic memory).
8. Let the child write, from memory, rhymes or pop songs familiar to him. This way he will be helped by the 'rhythm' of the task.

TO TEACH/CORRECT LETTER FORMATION

Handwriting practice should not last long but should be done regularly. Two good half-hour sessions a week will allow time for the child to learn to feel the movements and for the teacher to supervise and correct. It is best to base any remedial work upon observation of errors in the child's free writing so that it relates to his own stage of development and special needs. Very often observation and analysis of all the children's work will identify a group who need help with a similar problem.

Which handwriting programme is the best?

Jarman (1977; 1982), as mentioned above, suggests that we use what he calls a basic 'modern hand'; this prepares a child for cursive handwriting. He believes that print script can be damaging because the movements are now flowing or joined and they have to be unlearned eventually. In Europe all children learn a cursive hand upon entry into school; possibly the British should follow this example.

Alternative methods of recording

The typewriter as a substitute pencil

Writing is a complex skill and like many other skills becomes more or less automatic with practice. Once handwriting becomes automatic we only need to monitor our writing skill visually every now and again and so can give more time and attention to thinking about what we want to write. Unfortunately, the child who has difficulty in developing a fluent hand will always be concentrating on letter formation at the expense of content, structure and spelling. A convenient analogy may be to compare handwriting with learning to drive a car. Think what it was like when learning; every movement had to be analysed and concentrated upon. Once past the driving test, changing gear soon becomes automatic and we can refine the skill. We may even be able to drive and navigate at the same time!

The child who cannot write efficiently because of poor motor or perceptual–motor coordination will benefit from the provision of a keyboard as a substitute pencil. At some point a decision has to be made, possibly on his behalf, to relieve him of his handwriting difficulty. Poor handwriting may be viewed by some professionals as a 'maturational lag' that he can be left to 'grow out of'. The physical act of handwriting can be over-valued at the expense of the communication of ideas and experiences.

The decision to provide a child with a keyboard for written work should not be taken lightly. No one wants to add to the load in the already full school bag or make the child feel even more different from his peers. The decision should be the result of a multiprofessional assessment of the child's needs. This assessment will usually identify a discrepancy between overall attainment and ability to communicate through the written word. As has been said before, the child may not be able to write for straightforward physical reasons (such as tremor) or because he has some degree of apraxia (p. 67). The provision of any aid must always take into account the educational level of the child, the requirements of the curriculum and the environment(s) in which it is to be used.

THE PRIMARY CHILD

Teachers may start to be concerned about a child's writing when he reaches six or seven years old and is about to move from the infant school into the more formal environment of the junior school. The fact that his writing is immature compared to that of the rest of the class will become obvious to both teacher and class-mates; how the difficulty is handled at this point will be very important. If it is ignored as a 'maturational lag', then by the time that the child reaches the second-year juniors the fact that he cannot write will be a minor problem compared to his poor behaviour, emotional outbursts and negative attitude towards work.

Some children may be overlooked if the school is following a 'developmental' or 'emergent' writing programme and structured handwriting lessons are not as regular as they should be. Although this approach to writing is without doubt best for the majority of children, the child with perceptual–motor difficulty will continue to 'babble' on paper, not knowing that his letters are poorly formed and that words should have gaps between them. The brain-injured child is often unable to learn through exposure; all tasks need to be carefully structured for him to succeed.

Once the decision to provide a keyboard has been taken, then various educational and practical issues need to be considered.

Which typewriter? The young child needs a typewriter with a 'jumbo' or primary typeface (Figure 5.2). When a key is struck the typed letter should be clearly visible on the platten.

Figure 5.2: A primary typeface

This is a primary typeface.
abcdefghijklmnopqrstuvwxyz.
ABCDEFGHIJKLMNOPQRSTUVWXYZ.

As the child may have poor muscle strength in addition to poor coordination, it should be electric. Usually the child is based in one room and the machine does not need to be portable, but there must be access to a suitable electric outlet and the positioning of the machine should not isolate the child from the group. This may mean some rearrangement of the furniture and careful organization of the flex.

It may be necessary to fit a guard over the keyboard to help the child with poor coordination to locate the correct key. Guards are not available for all makes of typewriter or computer but they can be made by making a template and cutting the guard out of thick Perspex. The guard can then be screwed to the machine or, if the case is metal, use magnetic strips glued to the Perspex. You will need a technician to assist you in this.

A very unsteady child may need the additional support of the following:

(a)   a hand-grip to steady asymmetrical movements (Figure 5.3);

Figure 5.3: Two types of hand-grip

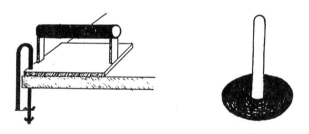

(b)   a wrist/elbow support to steady hand movement or support weak shoulder muscles (Figure 5.4);

Figure 5.4: Wrist and elbow support

(c)   a copy holder (available from many large stationers): this is best placed immediately above and behind the keyboard so that when copying the child only has to look up and down.

Seating. As with handwriting, attention should be paid to a child's sitting position when working at a keyboard. The back should be supported, the feet flat on the floor, and the machine on a table that allows leg room but also allows the child to work with no less than a 90° angle at the elbows. This will allow the child to see what he is doing and will not tire his arms. If the child only has functional use in one hand, the typewriter should be off-set to that side. This attention to detail is possible in the primary class, where the machine may be able to remain in one position, but is very difficult to sustain in the secondary school where the child moves from class to class and no table is the same height.

At the time of writing it is unrealistic to suggest any one machine that is suitable for primary use. Many machines currently in use in primary schools are now out of production. Up-to-date information on suitable 'jumbo' typewriters can be obtained from the CENMACH telephone information and advisory service.

Teaching keyboard familiarity. Many teachers assume that if a child needs a typewriter, then he will also have to learn how to touch-type. This, however, is *not* the main priority in providing a typewriter as a substitute pencil and this cannot be stressed strongly enough. The motor impaired child may not have the use of both hands; he may not have the coordination needed in both hands. He may not know his letter names and sounds, and he most certainly won't be able to spell very well. To impose the structure of a touch-typing programme will build in failure from the start. However, if the child's main problem is visual, then it would be valuable to follow a programme such as *Type It* (Duffy, 1974), which is discussed later in this chapter.

Each child has to be treated as an individual and the teaching method adapted to their particular abilities. For the young child it is more important that he should become familiar with the layout of the keyboard so that he can access keys quickly and understand the function keys (space, shift, etcetera) in order to use the typewriter independently in class.

The Goad method. Mrs Goad was a teacher in an ILEA school for children with a physical disability. Her proposal was that the keyboard is too confusing for the child who has perceptual and spatial difficulties. Her system (available from CENMACH) colour codes each row of letters and then the keyboard is covered with a thin piece of card. One by one, each letter is exposed by cutting holes in the card, and the child learns letter shape, position, sound and name by repeated use of each key over an appropriate outline drawing. The outline drawings are then collected in an initial sounds book and, once the keyboard has been completed, are labelled by the child to form his first picture dictionary. For many children, this is the first tidy piece of writing or the first realistic picture that they feel is theirs and the self-fulfilling aspects of the exercise are considerable.

Mrs Goad suggested that the child should start with the first letter on the middle row and progress along this row (green) to the top row (red) and finally to the bottom row (blue). This level of structure does work well with the less able child. However, in our experience, mainstream teachers prefer to first expose those letters that are meaningful to the child, possibly those in his name. As with any teaching 'method', it is only as good as the way in which it is introduced and maintained, and teachers should feel free to adapt the basic method to suit the child and their methods of teaching. Again, if the child has a visual difficulty, black-on-white letters will be better than three colours. If the school is following an 'emergent writing' approach, there is no reason why the child should not be allowed to remove the card mask at some point and 'babble' on the keyboard.

For the child who is already reading and spelling the same method is followed but short words are built up in place of the pictures.

The child is encouraged to use both hands if this is possible and to be aware of the mid-line on the keyboard, but we find that, given regular practice, the child will develop an individual style using those fingers that feel most natural. Some children choose to stabilize their hands by hooking their thumbs under the keyboard at the front; they then type with the index and middle fingers.

Ideally, the Goad Method should be presented at first on a regular daily basis with the child withdrawn from class. Ten or so minutes a day will ensure that the child quickly becomes independent on the typewriter and can use it freely in the classroom for all 'written' work. Handwriting and related pencil skills should continue. We have found that once the pressure to write has been removed, the child's pencil control may improve. In a very small number of cases the child has then elected to continue to write in the conventional way.

THE SECONDARY CHILD

Some children are not identified as poor writers until they approach secondary transfer. Until then a child may have been able to keep up with the demands upon him to write clearly by being allowed to work slowly or at his own pace. Suddenly, the teacher introduces copying from the board and the child cannot do this or work at speed. After a year in the secondary school the same difficulties may appear when the child's writing deteriorates under the additional pressures of speed and quantity of written work, and the different expectations of a range of teachers. Difficulties may also arise when using a wider range of drawing instruments and technical apparatus as in maths, science and CDT. Very often the subject-based secondary school teacher will be the one to identify a child's specific abilities and be the first to say: 'He's an able lad — pity he can't get his ideas down on paper'.

Which typewriter? To help the top junior child through the trauma of moving up and on, it is best to introduce the typewriter he will need to use at secondary school well in advance of the transfer date. Moving schools is difficult for any child but even more so for the youngster who may have difficulty with stairs and crowded corridors or who will be using his typewriter for the first time amongst strangers. If speech is poor, he will also have to learn how to communicate all over again with class-mates and staff, who may not be as accepting as those in the primary school. A writing aid must therefore be lightweight, unobtrusive, silent, independent of mains electricity and, ideally, have additional mathematical signs and symbols, and the facility for typing in a foreign language.

Technology in this field is moving very quickly and it is possible that by the time this book is published a smaller, lighter, more powerful typewriter will be available than we are using now. In ILEA, 'mainstreaming' for many children became a possibility because of the availability of electronic type-writers such as the Canon Typestar range (Canon (UK) Ltd.); currently, sec-ondary mainstream children are using the Typestar 90. The reasons for choosing this machine are many; they are outlined below to illustrate the criteria we have proved important.

1. It is portable, and a mains adaptor charges an internal battery pack. A ten-hour charge will last about three days.
2. It is lightweight, will fit into a school bag and is relatively silent in use.
3. Paper feed is automatic: for the child with very poor coordination computer print-out paper can be used so that once loaded the paper will not run out during a lesson.
4. A guard is available (Special Access Systems, Oxford) and Canon provide a good after-sales service.
5. All functions can be accessed using one finger only.
6. It has a 32-character, liquid-crystal display (LCD) that allows the child to edit text before printing out.
7. It has a memory of 6,000 characters [three full A4 pages] that can be divided into 26 separate 'files'. The child can type class notes into the memory and then correct and edit these in his own time before print-ing out. An additional RAM cartridge (4, 8 or 16kB) will enlarge the memory and is essential for the child who is about to start course work for the GCSE.
8. If the child has poor speech the visual display is just large enough for a question or answer to be typed in and be available for the teacher to read as she moves around the class. This saves valuable teaching time and reduces the disruption that has been known to occur whilst a child struggles to make himself understood.
9. The typewriter will print out in two different letter sizes (Figure 5.5).

Figure 5.5: The Canon Typestar 90 typefaces

This is the regular size typeface.

This is the larger typeface.

We are finding this valuable for children who have poor vision. Unfortunately the size of the letters in the LCD cannot be changed.

10. The typewriter has facilities for typing in up to five foreign languages; it also has a built-in calculator.

We have found the Canon 'teacher friendly' and both socially and educationally acceptable. Although there are smaller machines on the market, the Canon is the only one that does not need a separate printer and so allows the teacher the same access to the child's classwork as would be available were he to be writing in an exercise book. In our opinion a machine that meets all these criteria is the most appropriate match to normal written communication.

Typing at speed. Some children manage to develop quite a speed despite their method of fingering, but if a child is introduced to the typewriter with very little time to go before the public examinations, the decision may be taken to introduce touch-typing skills as a separate 'lesson'.

Most makes of computer have their own typing-tutor software and children seem to respond well to these especially if a self-competitive element has been built into the program. Some may elect to practise during their breaktimes and, if they are so motivated, it is important to allow them access to the computer. For top junior and lower secondary children we suggest a linguistically orientated typing program *Type It* (Duffy, 1974). About this, Joan Duffy writes:

> *Type It* is a linguistically orientated typing manual. It aims to strengthen fine-motor coordination, muscle (finger) strength and tone, eye–hand coordination, visual discrimination and visual memory. The manual is constructed to reinforce the spelling patterns of the phonetically regular words in our language as presented in the linguistic readers used by many classroom and special class teachers. As a beginning course in touch system typing, *Type It* has been used successfully with a variety of students ranging in age from 6 years to 22 years.

If the child has visual difficulties you may need to photocopy each sheet of the manual because the print is a pale brown and not very clear. Children who have difficulty keeping their place on a page also need the sheets to be copied and then cut up into small assignments and stuck onto cards. When working with a younger child you will reach the point when you have covered all the key letters and the practice words are not meaningful. At this point it is best to abandon that program and create your own practice sheets with words that relate to the child's current experiences.

For the older student who can only use one hand we suggest *Typewriting exercises for one-handed people (Kempthorne, 1978).*

Making the best use of the typewriter

RECORDING FACTS OR CREATIVE WRITING?

For many children with a motor impairment the use of a typewriter v 'll still be a physical as well as an intellectual effort. The amount of factual information that needs to be recorded may leave the child with little energy when it comes to creative writing. The following ideas are current practice in special education and could well benefit the mainstream child. However, persuasion may be needed to convince some teachers that to bend the rules concerning the way in which a task is carried out does not necessarily detract from the elements to be eventually learned.

1. Files are used rather than exercise books to reduce the weight the child will need to carry in one day and to allow the insertion of duplicated sheets where possible. Typed work can be given in for marking in plastic folders.

2. The teacher allows the child a copy of his own lesson notes or asks another child to make a copy of any notes taken in class and share them with the motor impaired child. The time and effort that would have been used in the physical act of copying are instead used to memorize or answer questions on the contents of the notes.

3. Notes or exercises with omissions are duplicated and the child supplies the key words or phrases. For some children — those with poor spatial judgement and poor hand control — typing onto a worksheet can be difficult. We suggest that each space on the sheet should be given a number and then the child makes a list of the omissions, matching them to the appropriate numbers. This is then placed opposite the worksheet in the file.

4. Questions are duplicated and inserted into the file to face the child's typewritten answers. Wherever possible, one-word or short-phrase answers are allowed.

5. Multiple choice answers to questions are provided and labelled with letters or numbers. The child only types the letter or the number.

6. The child is taught key-word note taking. From this list he can then write more fully in his own time.

7. As an alternative to note taking, the child needs access to resources such as tape-recordings, videos, slides, etcetera to use for revision purposes.

8. Diagrams and maps can be duplicated and important facts or labels added; this is better than a poorly executed drawing.

9. Sums can be duplicated so that the child only has to supply the answers. Large-key calculators can be used where appropriate (for example, Eurocalc SD815B; GLC Supplies, London).

10. Use a tape-recorder to encourage imaginative work by those children whose written composition is limited because of the physical effort involved — for example, those with muscular dystrophy.

THE POWER OF THE WORD-PROCESSOR

When we first introduced children to typewriters with word-processing (correction and memory) facilities, our priorities were ease of use and portability. Very soon it became apparent that creative teachers were using these facilities as a powerful teaching aid for children whose motor impairment was complicated by poor literacy skills.

A reluctance to put words on paper, poor spelling and sentence construction and poor concentration are not conducive to the production of 'at least half a page of writing before break'. If we are lucky, the motor impaired child with additional learning problems may manage one sentence. This will be full of mistakes; it will stay in the exercise book as a terrible reminder of yet another failure or, if typed or written on paper, it will most likely get lost by the next session. It is remarkable how little finished work these children ever have available to show!

If using a typewriter such as the Canon, the child should be encouraged always to type into the machine's memory. The completed sentence can then be printed out as a first draft but also stored for correction at a later stage. The child can be trained to look at the print-out and identify those words he thinks are not spelt correctly. Many children can do this quite well even though they cannot build words from scratch. These words can then be corrected on paper, and the child can recall his work from the memory and correct it with the word-processing facility. He may add a little to it and repeat the process of printing out and correcting. Little by little, literacy skills will improve, the length of the piece of work will be acceptable and the finished copy/final draft will be something to be proud of.

However, this process can take more than his fair share of teacher time and so it is important to develop the child's independence. One individual support teacher (Mrs. L. Rahamin, ILEA) devised a plan to encourage independence in a ten-year-old boy (Figure 5.6). The plan was stuck on a piece of card kept beside the typewriter as a reminder. By following this plan he was able to produce pieces of work as in Figure 5.7, something that would have been impossible had he not had the use of a typewriter with these facilities.

Figure 5.6: Planning for independence on the typewriter

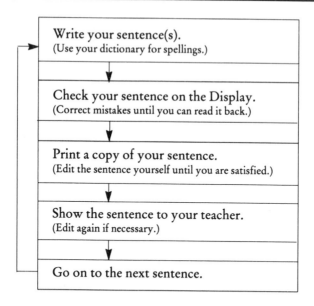

Write your sentence(s). (Use your dictionary for spellings.)
Check your sentence on the Display. (Correct mistakes until you can read it back.)
Print a copy of your sentence. (Edit the sentence yourself until you are satisfied.)
Show the sentence to your teacher. (Edit again if necessary.)
Go on to the next sentence.

A FEW PRACTICAL CONSIDERATIONS

Teacher attitudes. Many teachers are afraid of machinery, especially any that looks like a computer. They will need support if they are to welcome such innovations.

Individual teaching. It is reasonable for a class teacher to say that she cannot spare the time to work individually with the child in the early stages of typewriter use. Our experience has shown that it is counter-productive to leave a typewriter in a classroom where there is no individual support teacher or classroom aide for the child in question. At secondary level, such provision will work if the head of Special Needs is willing to take responsibility for educating the rest of the staff and for organizing such things as storage and security, as well as overseeing the progress of the child.

Security. Like any school equipment that is expensive, a typewriter should be security marked by whoever is responsible for this within the school. Parents should be advised to add the typewriter as a named item to their existing household insurance policy. The additional premium is minimal, and the typewriter is an important aid to daily living for their child. This covers the typewriter whilst it is in transit between home and school, which is when it is at its most vulnerable.

Figure 5.7: Using the memory facility for drafting pieces of work

---

TESSELLATIONS

I made a kite shap on a peg board and then I did same more and it
made a paten that will theet to gafe

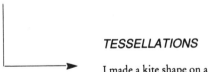

TESSELLATIONS

I made a kite shape on a peg board. Then I did some more and
it made a pattern that I joined together.

TESSELLATIONS

I made a kite shape on a peg board. Then I did some more and
it made a pattern that joined together.

TESSELLATIONS

I made a kite shape on a peg board. Then I did some more and
it made a pattern that joined together.
I cat out the shapes that I wanted printed.

TESSELLATIONS

I made a kite shape on a peg board. Then I did some more and
it made a pattern that joined together.
I cut out the shapes that I wanted printed.

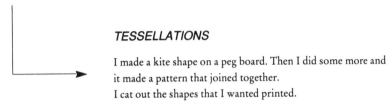

TESSELLATIONS

I made a kite shape on a peg board. Then I did some more and
it made a pattern that joined together.
I cut out the shapes that I wanted printed. I then stick them on
a piece of paper.

TESSELLATIONS

I made a kite shape on a peg board. Then I did some more and
it made a pattern that joined together.
I cut out the shapes that I wanted printed.
I then stuck them on a piece of paper.
I rolled ink over it, put paper on the top and took a print off it.

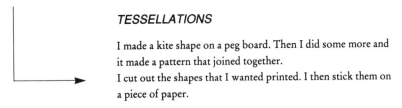

Storage. Heavy typewriters are not as easily stolen as the lighter and more portable variety; nor are they easy to lock away if it means carrying them some distance to the visual aids/computer room. We find that a locked cupboard in a classroom is adequate for both storage and security.

For the lightweight portable typewriter we suggest the child gets into the habit of leaving it in the school office during breaks and at the end of the day if it does not have to go home for homework.

Typewriters such as the Canon do need to be charged every so often. The mains adaptor for this has a plastic earth pin that breaks easily and so it is best if this is kept in one place, either at home or in school, and is not carried around.

Maintenance. The child should be encouraged to take care of his typewriter; he should understand from the start that it is his means of access to the mainstream curriculum. Other children in the class need to have its importance to that particular child explained. It is a mistake to think that by not allowing everyone to share it, little Ben will be 'different'. He will be even more different if he can neither write like the rest of the class nor type because his machine is continually at the menders after misuse by the other children.

Typewriters should be kept covered when not in use; dust and chalk will otherwise collect between the keys and jam them. The manual should be available and consulted before any attempt is made by an enthusiastic do-it-yourselfer to correct faults. Apart from damaging the machine, any tampering may make the guarantee void. A firm such as Canon, with good after-sales service, has a member of staff whose brief it is to deal with educational/disabled users.

Portability. As has already been discussed, the child who is very unsteady on his feet will need to have a backpack with semi-rigid shoulder straps to carry his books in. This will leave one hand free to carry the typewriter and the other to grab wall or bannister. Some teachers have tried to organize a rota so that a child's peers will help him to move around the school. This usually starts well but children are naturally forgetful, the novelty wears off and resentment could grow once this becomes a chore. Most children will be able to manage by being allowed to leave class a little earlier; some are able to carry their typewriter in a regular school bag.

Using the computer

Like the keyboard of a typewriter, the computer keyboard allows pupils to concentrate on the task of putting letters and words together without having to cope with the problem of drawing each letter. To use computer talk, we could say that the keyboard is a *menu* of pre-drawn shapes the machine can offer the pupil. Keyboard plus software can offer ready-made word lists, letter combinations, phrases and paragraphs that a child can make use of in a piece of writing. The computer allows the child to correct and alter his work as often as he likes without making a mess; the pupil is encouraged and motivated to create a print-out, which, however short, will always look good.

Likewise, the computer can offer help with art work from its menu of correctable, pre-drawn shapes; if a colour printer is available this is an added bonus. The child is free to experiment with combinations of shapes, something he cannot do with a pencil.

The computer will also allow the child to use a range of alternative devices to access the software. The most severely handicapped child will need to use a switch but the majority of children with minimal motor impairment can manage a keyboard (possibly with a guard), a concept keyboard, or a 'mouse'.

For the many children with a physical impairment who also have communication difficulties, the computer will allow both printed and spoken output. It can also transmit written messages by telephone and, if necessary, control other appliances.

Without support from centres specializing in software for special educational needs, most teachers have to select their software from what is already available in the school, or they are left to their own devices to search through catalogues. In selecting and designing appropriate software, we have found the elements described next to be of the utmost importance.

SPEEDING UP THE WRITING PROCESS

The provision of whole words that the child is able to select from a *word list*. This facility not only speeds up the writing process but allows the child to use words he could not spell correctly if he had to produce them letter by letter.

A list of words for use by a pupil could be a jumbled sentence, a set of words associated with a concept-keyboard overlay, a topic-based list, a concept-based list as in a thesaurus, or a list of words in alphabetical order. This list would be prepared in advance by the teacher.

Some programs, such as MAC Apple and Big MAC, which were originally written for the most severely handicapped, will automatically do things that both speed up writing and also make the finished work look so much more professional. For example, after a full stop the computer will make two spaces and the next letter will be a capital. After a comma, there will be one space. A 'u' will automatically follow a 'q'.

DIFFERENT METHODS FOR SELECTING

The way in which the child selects letters, words or shapes to be used in a piece of writing or drawing will depend upon both his motor control and the nature of the software. The motor impaired child in mainstream school will most likely be able to manage a keyboard, possibly with a guard, and a concept keyboard. But, surprising though it may seem, a 'mouse' and a true 'joy-stick' tend to require more dexterity than a pencil. The child has to grip the 'mouse' and move it across a flat surface until the moving arrow on the screen locates the desired letter, word or shape. He then has to steady the 'mouse' and press a switch. This is extremely difficult for the child with poor coordination. It is now possible to separate the switches from the body of the mouse in switch boxes available from CENMACH, and as a result many more children are experiencing success with software that can only be accessed in this way. Good seating and arm support is, of course, crucial.

IDEAS FOR SOFTWARE

The computer programs described in the next subsections are most certainly not an exclusive selection. Already there is memory-resident software that stores and sorts frequently used words and then offers them automatically to the writer when the first one or two letters have been typed. The chosen programs here illustrate the points discussed above, especially with regard to the ready-made elements such as word lists, which help to speed up the writing process. Of necessity, this software reflects the range of computers available to the children for whom we are responsible. It is hoped that the reader will be able to identify the important elements that will help the motor impaired child and so search for these when selecting software to match their particular computer system.

WRITING PROGRAMS

Ted. A simple word processor with word-list, which allows the child to edit, save and print text. It also provides small dictionaries from which the child can select whole words. The dictionaries have to be prepared by the teacher, are short (72 words) and can only be used one at a time. This program is available from the Inner London Educational Computing Centre (ILECC) for use on the 380Z, 480Z and Nimbus.

Big MAC. This program allows the pupil to produce, save, print and read text. The text is displayed and printed in both large and ordinary-size font.

On screen both the colour of the writing and the background can be changed to suit individual preference. It provides 20 short word-lists, each containing up to 54 words or phrases, which are prepared by the teacher and can only be used one at a time. It also has a long word-list (up to 1,000 words or phrases), which can be expanded by the child or the teacher and which can be used to supplement the short word-list. If a voice synthesizer is available, the text can be 'read out' word by word or letter by letter.

Selection of the letters and words can be made from the keyboard or by means of switches (or 'mouse' on the Nimbus version). Big MAC is aimed at developing writing skills in all children but, because of the nature of its special features, it is most appropriate to the needs of children with motor and visual difficulties.

A fuller description of this program's many facilities is available from CENMACH. Big MAC is available for use on Apple or Nimbus.

GRAPHICS PROGRAMS

Paint. This is a program that allows the creation of pictures and patterns. The teacher or child can store up to 15 picture elements, which can then be drawn and combined anywhere on the screen. Pictures and picture elements can be saved. There is a version that uses the concept keyboard available from ILECC for use on the 380Z and 480Z.

Carol. This program allows pictures to be created, saved and printed; text can be included in the picture. A limited range of standard shapes and operations can be selected from a menu by means of the arrow keys. The most recent version for the 480Z allows selection by a 'mouse'. Available from ILECC for use on the 380Z and 480Z.

PC Paintbrush. A powerful graphics program offering a range of operations and of modifiable standard shapes. Text can be added in a variety of styles and sizes. It is a 'mouse'-only program that makes use of both 'mouse' switches; therefore for some children a modified 'mouse' would be necessary. Available from Research Machines Ltd. (Oxford) for use on the Nimbus.

Logo and the turtle. Logo is a simple but powerful programming language that allows the user to 'teach' the computer more and more complex procedures. It can be used with a floor 'turtle' controlled by the computer, and thus becomes both a drawing instrument and a means of exploring the environment. For children with a motor impairment who have had little chance to explore their environment fully, the 'turtle' is a valuable learning tool as they are able to figure things out by placing themselves in the position of the 'turtle' and, through language, develop both spatial and geometrical concepts.

SEVERELY PHYSICALLY HANDICAPPED CHILDREN

Children who are unable to use a keyboard and who would access software by way of individualized micro-switches are now able to use a wide range of computer software. However, the provision of appropriate switch access and the teaching and learning processes involved are highly specialized and beyond the brief of this book. For information on local centres which will support individual children, contact CENMACH.

Social communication aids

It is most likely that a child with severe physical handicap will have limited or no speech. Cerebral palsy, or damage to the brain as the result of an infection or trauma are, as we have seen, the most usual causes. A child with a minimal motor impairment may have limited or very unclear speech which will only be understood by someone who is used to listening to him. His ability to make friends may be sadly limited.

The child's speech therapist would usually be responsible for suggesting and/or choosing an appropriate augmentative communication aid. Her choice will depend upon the child's age and interest level, his intellectual level and his physical ability to access the aid. It should also depend upon the school environment. A child may be able to communicate efficiently through signing within a signing environment at home or in a special school but may be very isolated in a mainstream school where only his helper can translate for him. The therapist may decide to refer the child to a Communication Aids Centre (CAC; for example, the Wolfson Centre, London) with a view to trying some of the most up-to-date portable speech synthesizers or to start him upon a symbol system.

It must be remembered that the most expensive equipment is not always the best solution. There are many aids to communication that supplement or replace speech and these range from simple picture charts to complex and expensive electronic equipment. Such aids vary greatly in terms of the skills required to use them. The child may need only to point to a series of pictures or symbols; or he may need to remember a series of codes. His motivation to communicate will therefore be important, as some of the more complicated aids take a lot of time and effort to use effectively.

Blissymbolics Communication (Spastics Society, Cardiff) is a visual-meaning based communication system designed to supplement the speech of children and adults who have severe speech and language disorders. Some of the symbols are pictographs, they look like the things they represent; others are ideographs, these represent ideas. Each symbol has the word written beneath. If the child is bilingual, both languages can be included. The advantage of '*Bliss*' is that anyone who can read can understand what the non-verbal person is trying to say. The system is not at all costly and when it wears out, new books or boards are easy to replace. Non-verbal children in London were introduced to the system over ten years ago and many still prefer to use their symbols rather than an electronic aid. They resist needing to use an alien voice, even though the newest communicators use a very sophisticated level of voice synthesis. A '*Bliss*' board can go everywhere with the child. It has no batteries to run out, and although it may take some time before the child develops a large symbol vocabulary and is able to combine these to communicate complex ideas, listeners need little or no training at all.

Blissymbols or word-boards remain the most portable methods of non-verbal communication, other than gesture or signing. Symbols are usually colour-coded and sorted into categories. A good user will store these in a display book with clear plastic pockets and be able to find his way quickly from one page to the next to send a telegram message. This message is then extended and expanded upon by the listener and so the conversation continues. The child may be able to indicate each symbol by pointing with the fist or finger; more severely disabled children may use a light-display or eye pointing.

If the child has very indistinct speech but is able to spell, then he may like to use the Canon Communicator (Canon (UK) Ltd.). This small machine can be strapped to the wrist or carried on a strap around the waist or over the shoulder. A mini-keyboard (available with plastic cover, in case the child dribbles, and guard for the poorly coordinated) will allow the child to print out messages on slim ticker-tape. It is especially convenient for the child who can make himself understood most of the time but may need to spell out key words. The Canon has rechargeable batteries and is therefore totally portable. The ticker-tape rolls are easy to replace if one follows the instructions inside the case carefully.

The range of portable communicators that may provide a visual display and a print-out (such as the *QED Memowriter*) or display, print-out and optional synthesized speech (such as *Lightwriter*) is continually being improved upon. Such machines are available from Easiaids Ltd. and the Foundation for Communication for the Disabled.

We would always advise that an electronic speech aid should be chosen by the child, the family and his speech therapist, after taking advice from a CAC and after trials of various pieces of hard- and software. It is all too easy to select a speech aid because it is familiar or readily available; cost may also influence choice. The wrong choice at any point can become an unused reminder of a costly error and a disappointed child.

A plastic identity card that can be carried at all times has now been designed for those who do not understand others or who themselves are not understood; for further information contact AFASIC.

Access to practical subjects

If the child with motor impairment is to take an equal part in lessons such as science, home economics, art, or CDT, additional planning will be necessary. With imagination and the will to find out what is needed and what is available, subject teachers should be able to accommodate the child. However, as discussed above, teachers are often afraid of taking responsibility for a child who they see as a safety hazard, not only to himself but also to the rest of the class. This is a realistic fear but one which can be relieved if the person involved is willing to start with an open mind.

The most valuable resource for any teacher of a practical subject is the nearest school for children with a physical disability. Here they will be able to talk with their opposite number who has experience of working with very severely disabled children; they will also be able to see gadgets that have been developed over the years in response to the needs of the physically impaired. As some of these aids are useful to anyone, not just the child in question, and are often so simple to make, we have known mainstream teachers to go away wondering why they have not thought of them before! A second resource is the occupational therapist, who will have access to a wide range of aids to daily living, which she may be able to loan on a trial basis. The Disabled Living Foundation has an information service and many publications dealing with access to a wide range of activities.

Parents will encourage the child; they may even insist the child plays a full part in the curriculum of the school but will then predictably and understandably over-protect him at home. The mainstream teacher may find that the child is unable to make a sandwich, boil a kettle or use a screwdriver. If this is so, then the child is further handicapped, not by his disability but by the misdirected caring adults who have inhibited him by nurturing a negative lethargy rather than a positive self-image.

Some teachers prefer to organize the class so that the child works with two or three friends who will complete those tasks he cannot manage. This may work well but very often the 'friends' do everything and their less physically adept class-mate sits and looks on. The judicious use of a classroom aide would be preferable.

A more positive approach is to look in more depth at each practical subject area and see what could be readily adapted to allow the child to take an equal part with his peers.

Science

Science so often provides the success that a child needs to motivate him to learn. It develops independence of thought as well as action and it helps children with learning difficulties to sequence ideas in a practical manner.

A useful book by Alan Jones (1983) will provide many ideas for classes at primary and lower secondary level. Each activity was chosen because it could be completed by a child who had to remain seated and who was capable of arm and hand movements similar to those required for feeding. Ideally the children should have a reading age of at least eight years, but if the teacher directs the activities this is not important. In other words, the child with a motor impairment should be able to do the same as everyone else.

However, the secondary curriculum assumes more formal activities and children need to use chemicals, heat sources and other specialized equipment. The following ideas may be useful in your particular situation:

DYCEM

This gelatinous material, described on p. 46, stays 'sticky' so long as it does not get too dusty. If this happens a wash in soap and water will refresh it. It is wonderful for stabilizing all sorts of things — paper on the table, flasks, etcetera. A strip stuck on the underside of a ruler will allow the child to position it and then draw along it without it shifting on the paper.

SOFTWOOD BLOCKS

Bottles of chemicals can be held steady in hollowed out and varnished softwood blocks to reduce spillages.

BURETTES

The stopcock on these is often small and the movement to open and close it has to be very precise. The handle can be enlarged as follows.

Take a piece of aluminium tube and cut a slot to half-way along its length. At the end of this cut, in the centre of the tube, work a small hole. Slip the cut end of the tube over the stopcock so that the handle runs along inside the tube. When it reaches the mid-point, fit the hole around the neck of the handle. Seal the cut tube and plug and cover both ends; electrical tape will do this and remain waterproof.

BUNSEN BURNERS

To stabilize the burner cut a circular hole the same size as its base in a piece of heavy hardwood. Ensure that the gas pipe is long enough to allow the child who is sitting to reach the appliance. Fix the burner into the wooden base and then place a tripod of suitable height over it. Drill holes for the legs and fix these into the base. The tripod acts as a guard for the flame. Two additional metal rods screwed into the base either side of the tripod can have a piece of wire attached that will encircle the flask or beaker and hold this steady (Figure 5.8).

Figure 5.8: Stabilizing a bunsen burner

DISSECTION

Simple dissections can be done by using a nail board to hold the specimen steady.

The child with very weak or unsteady arm and hand muscles may benefit from working on a Perspex 'trolley' with a hole cut in the middle (Figure 5.9). The hands are held clear of the dissection yet the window and the castors allows easy movement over the work. A sheet of Dycem under the castors will limit unwanted movements.

MICROSCOPES

The regular school microscope is difficult to use because the eyepiece is at the wrong angle, individual slides are difficult to manipulate, and the coarse-focus knob may be difficult and stiff. The school may have the use of a microprojector that allows whole groups to view prepared slides but if not,

Figure 5.9: A Perspex board to support the elbows during dissection

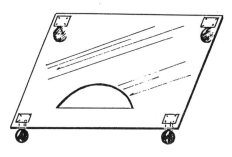

there is a wide range of magnifiers available (Philip and Tacey Ltd.) designed for use with young children, who also find coordination difficult.

Craft, design and technology

WOODWORK

A mitre saw (Mobilia Systems) is a piece of equipment that will both hold the wood to be sawn in place and hold the saw steady so that the child only has to move it back and forth to cut the wood. This allows even the most uncoordinated child a degree of success and could also be useful in teaching the correct sawing motion to other children. Other aids include a dovetailing guide and a chiselling guide (RNIB).

Whether or not the child succeeds in this area will depend very much upon the complexity of the task. Cutting sections off a thick dowel-rod (broom handle) to sand and paint and turn into draughts or chess pieces, and painting squares on a board with the aid of a stencil will be more valuable to some children than struggling with an intricate joint. For the child who cannot manage to work large, a project could be broken into small components and then reconstituted.

A shadow board, made by painting the silhouettes of the tools on a sheet of peg board, means that the children can store their tools safely and correctly.

TECHNICAL DRAWING

We suggest that children use one of the portable drawing boards with horizontal rule, vertical scale and angle protractor (for example, Draft-Ease, Hellerman). The board has simple locking mechanisms, ideal for the child with poor motor control; an air brush (Devilbiss Co. Ltd.) is useful for shading exercises.

Photography

Many children could enjoy this activity but are unable to hold the camera steady. This can be solved if a tripod is used with a remote-control shutter release. The child in a wheelchair can have the camera attached to his chair with the Mobilia range (Mobilia Systems) of adjustable clamps. For further information, contact the Disabled Photographers Society.

Art

No longer does success in this area depend upon the ability to draw an object in minute detail. Most cutting, sticking and pasting techniques, printing and stencil work, or taking rubbings of natural objects, all rely for their success upon the creative eye rather than the steady hand. We have had children create Christmas cards on an electric typewriter (Figure 5.10), and the possibilities for computer art are growing every day. SHAPE London is an organization that develops and expands the ways in which people with disabilities can enjoy and participate in the arts in the London area.

Home economics

Most children enjoy cooking and many do not get the chance to experiment at home. The child with a motor impairment is most likely seen as a 'disaster area' when it comes to the family kitchen and yet they, like any other person, need to be able to look after themselves at some point, if only to make a simple nutritious meal. A useful book, which considers the importance of kitchen design, provides ideas for the adaptation of cooking utensils and suggests simple recipes, is available from the Disabled Living Foundation (1976; see below).

Figure 5.10: Using the typewriter to create a Christmas card

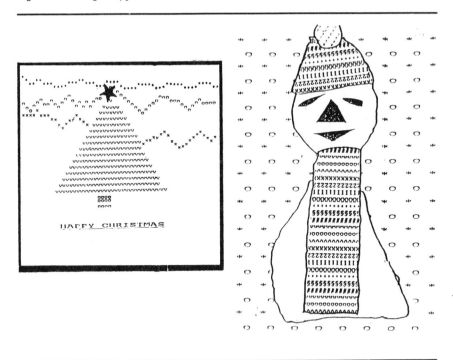

Apart from the availability of a sheet of Dycem matting, a few things that may prove of immediate help to the child with a motor impairment are as follows:

A TROLLEY (FIGURE 5.11).

A sturdy trolley will double as a walking aid. The type illustrated here also has a built-in 'ramp' so that heavy objects can be slid from one surface to another. Even a light, folding trolley will be of help to a child who cannot balance and carry dishes very easily (see description in *Kitchen Sense for Disabled or Elderly People*; Disabled Living Foundation, 1976).

A SPIKE BOARD (FIGURE 5.12)

This is especially useful for a child with the use of one hand only. One can be made very easily by hammering a pattern of nails through a piece of board. Use long nails if you wish to hold large objects, such as vegetables, steady, and smaller ones for meat. Stabilize on a sheet of Dycem.

Figure 5.11: A trolley for the Home Economics room

Figure 5.12: Peeling vegetables with one hand on a spike board

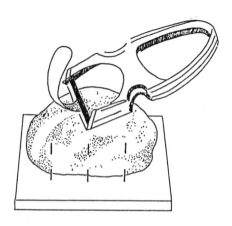

A SPREADING BOARD

This is especially useful for a child with the use of one hand only. Nail half-inch, quarter-round beading to two sides of a board. A piece of bread or a biscuit can then be pushed against the raised sides for spreading. Stabilize on a sheet of Dycem.

CHOPPING AND PEELING

Use an 'onion stick' or the spike board to hold vegetables steady whilst they are cut with a knife. Use scissors for herbs, chopping the leaves up in a cup. To peel a potato or other root vegetable, place it on the spike board and use a double-edged cutter, which can be used by either hand.

OPENING JARS, BOTTLES AND CANS

The 'Onduit' (Hestair Hope, Oldham) is a simple metal plate with a raised 'V' shape, the inside rim of which is serrated. This is fitted onto the underside of a shelf. A child with one hand can hold the jar up against the 'V' and twist the lid open.

A square of Dycem will provide the leverage necessary to open a stiff bottle top.

A wall-fitted can opener, with a shelf beneath that will adjust to the height of the can, allows the child to position the can and open it by turning the handle.

Sewing

It may be that the only barrier to child being totally independent in sewing is that he cannot thread the needle because of poor motor coordination or perceptual difficulty. The Perfecto needle threader (Nottingham Rehab) allows needles to be threaded at the touch of a button. Needles of different sizes should also be considered, as should the type of fabric being used. Binka and other large-weave materials are easier to hand sew than slippery synthetics. If handling skeins of embroidery thread is a problem, then transfer the thread to empty cotton reels, preferably the ones with a slim stem and thicker end-pieces. The Nottingham Rehab catalogue holds a range of aids to making sewing easier for the motor impaired, and the Disabled Living Foundation will be able to advise on adaptations to electric sewing machines for those who cannot use foot pressure. Many children will find an old hand-sewing machine much easier to manage.

Teachers may like to get in touch with a new fashion service that has been set up to produce fashionable clothing to meet the individual needs of people with a physical disability and allow for maximum independence in dressing and care. Fashion Services for the Disabled incorporates a training centre, which offers courses to teachers of dress to give them a greater understanding of disability. Many youngsters with a motor impairment will not have the same opportunities to go out to the shops as their friends, so their wardrobe may be limited and inappropriate; they should be encouraged to make their own clothes. Looking to the future, most will need to find employment of a sedentary nature and dressmaking could be one way in which they could earn a living. The Disabled Living Foundation (Bumphrey, 1981) also sells a publication entitled *Dressmaking for the Disabled*.

Music

If a child has difficulty in playing an instrument because of his motor impairment, teachers may like to contact REMAP, who will help in adapting musical instruments to meet individual needs. A useful book, which includes a section on adapting instruments, is *They Can Make Music* by Paul Bailey (1973). He also describes how to adapt traditional techniques to meet the needs of weak hands or poor muscular control.

Left-handers

A wide range of kitchen utensils, household items and educational aids designed for left-handed children is available from Lefties, a company set up to respond to the specific needs of the left-handed.

Chess and other table games

If magnetic boards are used and counters adapted, either enlarged, weighted or magnetized, it is quite possible for children with poor coordination to join in the normal range of table games. Chess for the physically impaired has been researched and the teaching method adapted for the less able (Agnew and Povey, 1984).

Physical education, movement, games and swimming

A motor impaired child's ability to take part in games and PE, movement or swimming is usually one of the first issues that is brought up in preliminary discussions about access to the curriculum. The new challenge facing the physical education profession is to integrate these children into regular lessons in such a way that they not only achieve success but also feel they are being successful. Like the other children the child with a motor disability has a right to receive physical education appropriate to his needs. Provided the medical limitations are fully understood and all necessary safety precautions taken, then he should be physically challenged and teachers should not be afraid to extend him. The teacher must take a positive attitude and discover abilities within the limits of impairment rather than focus on disabilities. A full range of activities is available to children in special education. This is because activities and apparatus have been adapted to suit their unique needs. A visit by mainstream staff to the local school for children with a physical disability is a very good starting point when it comes to planning for the inclusion of the motor impaired child.

In mainstream schools the integration of motor impaired children into PE, movement and swimming is a relatively straightforward process. The children may have to work in twos or threes but the teaching approach and the nature of the activity focuses upon the individual (KCC.ED, 1986). The teaching of games presents a bigger problem, especially in the secondary school where the basis of the activity is to cooperate within a team and to compete against others. The mainstream teacher should refer to Alan Brown's comprehensive book *Active Games for Children with Movement Problems* (Brown, 1987), which covers the subject thoroughly. He maintains that within any games lesson there may be different degrees of integration. Whereas all children may be integrated into the skills training part of the lesson, and into small group practices where the games are appropriately adapted, when it comes to team games where competition is involved, the less able members may still be able to gain satisfaction from an active role as umpire, scorer or team coach (p. 112).

The ideas presented here are intended to raise general issues of organization and teaching method and to provide a stimulus for discussion and further research.

Is the activity safe?

It is very important that the teacher is aware of the child's impairment and understands what effect this may have upon his performance in certain activities. It is advisable that she takes time to talk to the school doctor, nurse or therapists to find out what she can expect the child to be able to do. Apart from taking a few sensible precautions, most children with any degree of impairment benefit enormously from the exercise, and from the 'hidden curriculum' implicit in the discipline and team-work involved. The nature of and approach to the following conditions has been considered in Chapter 3; recapitulation here is of essentials.

ARTHRITIS

The physiotherapist will advise on suitable activities and possibly try to incorporate therapy into PE lessons.

ASTHMA

Attacks may be provoked by exercise, especially on cold, dry days. This may be prevented by ensuring that the child takes a tablet or uses his inhaler about 20 minutes before the lesson. This condition should not be used as an excuse to get out of PE. Success usually encourages confidence. Swimming is especially beneficial.

BRITTLE BONES

Remember that a fracture in school, unless it is caused by negligence, is not the fault of the teacher. These children benefit greatly from swimming and other non-weight bearing exercises.

CEREBRAL PALSY

If we consider that the effort needed to sustain a 'wobbly' walk is equal to that which the able-bodied child would need were he to run everywhere, then we can understand that the child with cerebral palsy is likely to get very tired and will need to be able to sit down whenever possible.

CONGENITAL HEART DEFECT

The doctor or parent will be able to tell you just how much he can or should be able to do.

DIABETES

To avoid an insulin reaction the child may need to have a snack before or during exercise to maintain his blood sugar levels.

EPILEPSY

If the child knows when a fit is about to start, he will be able to get himself into a safe position or alert a partner. The degree of one-to-one supervision needed will depend on the advice of the doctor and the wishes of the parent. Close supervision when swimming is advisable.

MUSCULAR DYSTROPHY

This area of the curriculum, more than any other, will highlight a child's progressive weakness. This is a situation that will need sensitive handling, as well as adaptations to equipment and activities introduced so that the child can be a full member of the group for as long as is possible.

SMALL STATURE

Again, physical activity can be exhausting; care should be taken not to put too much stress on already abnormal joints or on the spine.

SPINA BIFIDA

The child will usually be able to compensate for weakness in the lower limbs by developing a strong trunk, shoulders and upper limbs. Consequently he may get himself into situations where he is unaware that he is doing damage to his lower limbs. If the child has hydrocephalus and a valve, care should be taken that he does not bang his head. Some children wear lightweight cycling helmets to guard against knocks.

If the motor impairment limits mobility, then the child may feel the cold more than most, especially as he may have to spend more time watching than being actively involved. Hypothermia is a real danger if the child has limited sensation in any limb.

Teaching implications

EQUAL OPPORTUNITIES

If the motor impaired child is to be a true member of the group, then he has to be able to share in any decisions concerning the adaptation of equipment and activities. Let him and his class-mates discuss the best and the most fair way to do this. Children are imaginative and, at times, scrupulously fair!

It may be possible to borrow wheelchairs so that all the class have the same 'handicap'. The children might be encouraged to use their non-dominant hand or foot, or to work with one arm tied behind their back. If handled correctly, simulating disability in this atmosphere can be an important influence upon attitude change.

Avoid allowing the other children to select teams in front of the whole class. Impaired or not, there are always children who are the last to be picked.

Try to avoid elimination games. So often it is the unskilled child, the one who needs the most practice, who ends up spending most time sitting on the sidelines. Make sure that there is enough equipment for each child so that no one has periods of inactivity.

Always comment on improved scores, not just the highest.

TEACHING BASIC SKILLS

For many children a motor skill will need to be broken down into its developmental sequence, and each stage taught and built upon to achieve the desired end. It is common practice in the world of sport to 'coach' the gifted, but not so usual for the less able to be given the same attention outside school hours.

In class, it may be possible to pair a skilled child with the motor impaired child; this way he has a good model to learn from. For example, in learning ball skills it is important that the ball is fed accurately. If two impaired children work together they will fail to make any progress because they cannot pass the ball accurately. The social benefits of mixed ability practice can be considerable because both children can share the pride of achievement. But the role of feed player must be rotated so that the able child does not miss out on his own development.

The importance of additional help in PE and games lessons must be mentioned. Another adult present can make all the difference to the success of an integrated activity. Most schools for children with a physical disability rely upon volunteers, and in mainstream it is often possible to recruit sixth-formers keen to do voluntary work in a free period.

THE SIMPLIFICATION OF PERCEPTUAL DIFFICULTIES

The child with a perceptual–motor difficulty will find working with balls especially difficult. Much can be done to help him visually track and respond to ball movement by modifying the flight of the ball, its size and its degree of bounce. Over-inflated bladders and beach balls tend to float in the air and thus slow down the response needed by the child. They are large and brightly coloured and so are easy to track. The degree of bounce can be reduced by using foam; low-bounce balls are now on the market. The ball service in a game can be reduced in difficulty and progressively graded as the skill improves. Practise rolling and bouncing, then underarm before overarm throwing.

Try to simplify and/or reduce the rules of the game and the number of decisions a child has to make within it.

THE SIMPLIFICATION OF MOTOR DIFFICULTIES (FIGURE 5.13)

Often the child with a motor impairment who is a poor walker will get more satisfaction out of the lesson if he is allowed to work in a wheelchair. If some children are in chairs it is possible to substitute walking or wheeling for the running parts of a game.

If distances are a problem, reduce the size of the playing area — decrease the length of the pitch or the distance from the child to the target. If a net is being used this can affect the speed of play: a high net slows a game down; a low net makes the game quicker but also makes throwing and batting easier.

Substitute light plastic apparatus (bats, hoops, etcetera) if grip and muscle strength is poor. Use bean bags in preference to balls; they are easier to grasp and release in throwing activities. Motor impaired children, and small children, are for ever losing the ball. Beach-type games, where the ball is attached by a string to a central, flexible stand, are ideal for batting practice.

CHOOSING APPROPRIATE ACTIVITIES

A motor impaired child's success at any activity will be determined first and foremost by the degree of disability. In mainstream, most will be able to take part in mat work, bench work, and some may even try the wall bars and ropes. Balance may be poor and they may need one-to-one supervision but this should not exclude them from PE. In games, their success will depend upon the match the teacher has been able to achieve by imaginative adaptation and upon the nature of the game. A child in a wheelchair will be able to play volleyball and basketball, netball or indoor hockey, but would find

Figure 5.13: The simplification of motor activities in the games lesson

football, cricket or rounders very difficult on the field. The fact that a child cannot take an active part in an activity does not mean that he cannot be involved. He may become the scorer or the umpire or the coach but to be able to do this job he needs to know and understand the rules and the tactics of the game, and so should not be excluded from the early stages of play.

The British Sports Association for the Disabled at Stoke Mandeville has a wide range of information on wheelchair sports, including archery, netball, swimming, athletics and javelin throwing. Through planning for activities that all can join in, it often happens that the games curriculum of the mainstream school is extended and enriched by the addition of some more unusual sports.

SWIMMING

Water allows mobility to many children who are otherwise physically limited. Stiff and paralysed limbs can float and move with the support of water and the absence of muscular control in the legs is not important. It is an activity that breeds confidence and is something that can be a hobby all through life. Gross motor activity has a positive effect upon fine motor skills and the exercise is good all round; it improves the circulation, supports active movement and allows the passive movements of the joints necessary to prevent contractures.

Special advice on teaching the young disabled child to swim is offered in the Association of Swimming Therapy's publication *Swimming for the Disabled*. In mainstream schools most children visit the local baths but care must be taken to ensure that the water is warm enough; if it is too cold it may cause an increase in spasm, which will make swimming impossible. Hypothermia is also a risk, especially if the child has no feeling at all in his legs. Because of his limited movement the child may be unable to right himself and so the wearing of any swimming aid should be closely supervised and advice should be sought from the physiotherapist before one is used.

Allowing a child to gain confidence in the water could open up the whole area of water-borne activities that are now becoming available for disabled persons. Special schools are already involved in sailing and canoeing programmes. Youngsters go on to enjoy adult involvement in projects such as SPARKS (RADAR, London), and sub-aqua diving is now enjoyed by many paraplegics who can still move well in the water.

If taking children on a school journey, do remember that the motor impaired child who is quite at home in the warm, calm waters of the local swimming pool may be unable to cope with salty, cold, and possibly turbulent water. It will be important to approach sea swimming slowly and sensitively so as not to crush his confidence.

6 Educational Implications of Motor Impairment
2. Associated Learning Difficulties

Figure 2.1 showed clearly that the motor impaired child may also have specific learning difficulties. However, not all children with a physical difficulty are affected, only those whose condition can be associated with a degree of brain damage. Those who have spina bifida and hydrocephalus, cerebral palsy or damage to the brain due to trauma or infection (Chapter 3) are the most likely to have trouble learning but each child's problems will be specific and we cannot make any generalizations. Some severely impaired children are highly intelligent and once given access to some form of communication are able to share that ability (Nolan, 1987), whereas the cerebral palsy child with only a slight limp and epilepsy may have enormous difficulty learning to read and spell.

When a young child with a motor impairment first arrives at a mainstream school the major difficulties appear to be those of management. As explained in Chapter 5, movement around the class and the school, access to a writing aid, practical activities, and physical care are all understandable issues and as such can be solved as quickly as possible, given the resources available to the school at that time. If the child is slow to develop language or acquire a sight vocabulary, or if he cannot spell even the most simple word and has no concept of number at all, this is far more difficult to deal with. To help children with such learning difficulties to succeed, the first task must be to define the problem as clearly as possible.

When describing learning difficulties it is all too easy to take what has been called the 'pessimistic' approach — one which assumes the problem is the result of the medical condition or of home background and that there is little the school can do about it. In special education, teachers tend to take an 'indirect' approach; this focuses upon assumptions about the underlying processes that affect learning, such as poor visual memory and perceptual–motor difficulty. In small classes with additional help and paramedical advice ready to hand it is easier to concentrate upon programmes that have been designed to train deficient skills.

The mainstream teacher, however, has no time for such luxuries. With 29 other children demanding her attention, little Benjamin is only entitled to one-thirtieth of her time, and so any attempt to cope with his specific learning difficulties has to focus upon his performance in context. A 'curriculum-based' approach will allow his difficulties to be described in terms relevant to teacher action and is optimistic in that it implies that change is possible.

Specific learning difficulties is a term that has been widely adopted for describing difficulties with visual and auditory perception and memory. It has been argued that any such theoretical definition is not appropriate for teacher action in that it does not help the teacher to decide what to teach. However, just as it is important to consider the effects of poor motor coordination upon learning, so is it important for the teacher to be able to understand which intellectual processes may be impaired as a result of brain damage. Perceptual theory, touched upon in psychology lectures at college, is difficult to understand out of context yet makes considerable sense when used to describe the specific difficulties of a child with spina bifida and hydrocephalus. An understanding of the possible reason for Ben's inability to remember initial sounds takes the guilt from the teacher who has been trying to teach these for a term without success. It also allows the teacher to look at the child's performance in real learning situations, to specify what he can and cannot do and then decide upon appropriate learning targets that relates to these tasks.

Identifying the problem areas

Attention

The first thing that the teacher may notice is that the child is easily distracted by what is going on around him and that his ability to stay 'on task' for more than five minutes is limited. It is not only general classroom activity that can distract him; whilst reading or writing he may stop to comment upon something else on his table, his clothes, even a tear in a page. Whatever it is he chooses will usually have little, if any, relationship at all to the task in hand. If working on counting and colouring activities he is quite likely to count the petals on the flower rather than the number of flowers in the picture, or he will colour the petals green. He makes little mistakes that can so easily be misinterpreted as 'being silly'. He will continually lose his place in his book and possibly start to work on a totally unrelated page if not supervised closely. Class teaching tends to flow past distractable children and subsequently learning is patchy. Neither will the child pay attention to the teacher's announcements and so will not know the plans for the day nor what he is supposed to do next. If a task is too difficult, the child may just 'switch off' and allow his attention to wander.

Try to keep the child from distracting both himself and others with irrelevant conversation. All talking should relate to the task in hand. This child learns best one-to-one or in a small group with the least possible distraction. This, of course, goes against the principles of integration and teachers are resistant to seating the child in a quiet 'bay' within the classroom in case he is made to feel 'different'. As has been said before, he will feel even more different when he does not learn to read and write like the rest of his friends. A compromise needs to be reached if the distractable child is going to achieve his potential. However, allowances should be made for the fact that the child will find it extremely difficult to concentrate for any length of time on one task. Allow half an hour on one area of study and then change direction. The child should understand this difficulty and be encouraged to monitor his own progress. The preparation of materials and subject matter should match the child's ability and interest levels.

Memory

In addition the child may have a poor short-term memory — difficulty in recalling what he has just been doing or what he has been told to do. He will find it difficult to learn by heart. It may be possible to determine (by the *Aston Index*; p. 71) whether the child's auditory memory is stronger than his visual memory, or vice versa. The outcome of this assessment will allow the teacher to work upon his strengths rather than his weaknesses. For example, if a child has a weak visual memory (common in spina bifida and hydrocephalus), it will be more difficult for him to remember written instructions. When asking him to follow a recipe or an experiment, verbal instructions or a verbal interpretation of the directions could thus help him to achieve more. Try highlighting the most important points to help the child focus on and attend to them. A good ploy is for the child to talk himself or his teacher through an activity.

At all times, instructions need to be short and simple; the child needs to be taken through activities one step at a time and repetition is the key to learning success. At the end of a lesson, take time to 'recap' on what has been learned.

Comprehension and language development

The child may be slow to absorb information. He may find it difficult to sort and classify, to see what belongs together. Some children may be quick to read but when questioned about content will not be able to answer appropriately. The child will need to be questioned closely about the sequence of events and outcome of the story. He may be helped through this if allowed to refer to a list of key words that relate to the content. Instead of giving instructions, ask the child to say how he thinks he should tackle a task and why he is going to do what he says he will.

Children who are slow to develop language may still only be using, and possibly understanding, short simple sentences. If the child's development of oral language is limited, he will not attempt long or complex sentences, his vocabulary will be limited, and this will make it difficult for him to anticipate the use of words in a sentence and so understand what he is reading. Poor auditory discrimination, so often associated with language difficulties, will affect the learning of the phonic skills needed for reading and spelling.

Children with unclear speech (dysarthria and dyspraxia; p. 24) may experience both social and educational difficulties in school. The young child does not usually realize that anything is wrong, but once in school he will become increasingly aware that he is not always understood by his teachers or his class-mates. His response to this difficulty will depend greatly upon his personality. Some will withdraw from contact with others; some will try to maintain a conversation but will 'switch off' once they realize they are not being understood; others may become verbally angry or physically aggressive. The fact that the child becomes a social isolate or suffers from teasing and bullying will severely limit the growth of his self-concept. Success in communication will usually be through his determination to make others understand and the positive response of others who admire his tenacity. Whether the child is a wit or highly intelligent will also affect this process.

The child's ability to develop an efficient communication system will depend greatly upon how his language difficulty is handled by the important adults in his life. The teacher needs to maintain a balance between not anticipating educational difficulties but using, from the start, teaching strategies that are likely to help any child with unclear speech. A home–school book will help parent, teacher and therapist to keep in touch and work together to help him. The child should be involved in regular small-group discussions led by an adult, so that he is helped to listen as well as to speak. Reading and writing skills need to be linked from the start, and paired reading as part of extensive exposure to books will promote reading as an enjoyable task. The learning by heart of songs, rhymes and jingles will build his confidence.

Sequencing

This is the process whereby we are able to place objects or events and abstract configurations in a temporal or spatial order. The prerequisites are recognition and comprehension. Some children cannot perform the various stages of a task in the correct order and so cannot complete it satisfactorily. They may be unable to organize the materials they will need and so cannot start on a task; they cannot plan ahead. This is first evident when the child tries to dress himself: he will put his clothes on inside out and back to front, possibly in the wrong order. This inability to organize can also affect thought processes; such children cannot think things out logically. Defective sequencing will affect both the child's abstract and concrete ability and, later, his literacy and numeracy skills. Some children with a motor impairment may learn to avoid having to reason through a problem by opting out and allowing someone else to make decisions for them. This should be watched for and discouraged.

In teaching a practical task the teacher may like to try 'backward chaining'. The child starts by finishing off an activity that has been started by the teacher. For example, in making a pot of tea, he would first be allowed to pour the tea out; he would then progress backwards through the task of putting milk in the cup, pouring water into the pot, measuring the tea, heating the pot and so on. This way the child slowly learns the correct sequence and always ends on a note of success.

Spatial and visual perceptual difficulty

These can affect the performance of any practical task because the hands and/or the body are required to move in space and because movement is structured by vision. The teacher may first notice that the child, either walking or in a wheelchair, cannot move about the classroom without bumping into people and furniture. This can cause social difficulties as well as being dangerous to all involved. If asked to find an empty space on the carpet or a spare chair, he will not find it without a prompt. Stairs and kerbs can be a terrifying experience. The child cannot judge the depth of the step and may stop short of the kerb when trying to cross a road. Handwriting will be untidy and, unless the child can work on lined paper, he will be unable to keep it in straight lines. The correct use of scissors may present difficulties, as this requires moving in two planes at once, not only chopping up and down but also squeezing from side to side. Scissors are available (Rompa) that only need an up-and-down movement, although most manage this skill eventually.

These children find it very difficult to extract information from a complex scene, whether this means looking at a picture for clues, understanding a diagram or following a map, or trying to cross a busy street. Spatial difficulty can prevent them from driving a car because they cannot see or recognize danger signals in complicated traffic. After school this difficulty may exclude them from certain types of work, especially if machinery is involved.

Children with spatial difficulties often respond well to colour coding. A colour-coded typewriter (Chapter 5) helps the child to learn the keyboard; a coloured dot placed at the start of a letter is an aid to correct letter formation. Some children need a dot on the left-hand top corner of the paper to remind them to start writing from that position. Colour can be used to emphasize the sequence on a worksheet, and it can be used as a directional aid in a building. For example, the teacher might send the child to the school office saying, 'Follow the blue wall until you see a red door, go through that and knock on the green door'.

Temporal difficulty

The child may have a very poorly developed sense of time; he will find it difficult to work within a set time limit. This is not only because he lacks a concept of time but also because associated difficulties, such as poor hand–eye coordination and visual/spatial problems, slow down his performance. He may not fully understand what is required of him; he may make mistakes whilst doing it and, being unable to think logically, he may do most of his work by trial and error. Some children, realizing their weaknesses, rush through their work just to get it over and done with. Either way, the results may not be very satisfactory.

The child needs extra time to practise new skills and should be given tasks he can reasonably be expected to complete in the time allowed. The self-fulfilling effects of success are always the best motivator.

Transfer of knowledge and skills

Often the skills taught at school are not generalized, either across the curriculum or across differing situations. The child may learn to add and subtract in class but will not be able to use this skill to adapt a recipe in cookery or handle money at the shops. It seems that the change in his environment is an important factor because often his performance improves once he has got used to the different situation and has understood the relationship between the basic skill and how to use it in real life.

Neurological or functional immaturity

Some children are slow to develop motor control. This must not be confused with the effects of muscular spasm, tremor or poor hand–eye coordination. If a child is watched carefully it will be obvious that the way in which he handles and controls tools is at the level of a three- or four-year-old. He may be unable to complete an activity if it means crossing the midline and will need to be talked through it. He may have problems with copying a peg-board pattern where there are diagonal lines. This sort of physical difficulty can be helped by teaching and plenty of practice.

Emotional barriers to learning

The child with both a motor impairment and learning difficulties has to work hard to keep up both socially and academically with his peers. The psychosocial implications of a physical disability will be considered more fully later in this book but it is relevant here to stress the implications for learning. The child will soon realize that he does not match up to his peers and, as a consequence, self-confidence and morale may suffer. The child who is afraid of failure may become over-anxious and eventually give up. Alternatively he may respond with erratic behaviour becoming explosive and over-reactive. Some children may have a unrealistic attitude towards their learning difficulties; they may or may not admit that they have problems but will still not understand why they cannot pursue a certain course of study or take up certain jobs. They will need careful counselling when it comes to a choice of career.

Medical issues

It must not be forgotten that the performance of the child will also be affected by his state of health, which may be more unstable than for most children. His physical difficulties may prevent him from sleeping well and may tire him by half-way through the day. He may have to spend long periods of time in hospital. The side-effects of drugs will also affect his ability to learn.

Visual and hearing impairment

Many children with a motor impairment also have, as discussed earlier, associated difficulties with vision or hearing. If either is suspected, then referral through the school medical officer should ensure that the child is tested and that suitable aids are provided. The school should then contact the specialist teacher, who will be able to advise the class teacher on the most appropriate teaching strategies for that particular child.

The effect of poor sensory and motor organization on basic educational attainments

In considering the effects of deficiencies in sensory and motor organization upon reading, writing, spelling and number work, we have to remember that a separate consideration of each skill is arbitrary and not meant to obscure the fact that in learning one skill the child is also influencing and being influenced by the others. Good teaching should ensure such interdependence.

The following are general comments intended to raise an awareness of the organizational difficulties that may be affecting a motor impaired child's progress in basic skill work.

Reading

Success in reading will partly depend upon flexibility in the child's sensory organization of both visual and auditory stimuli. Of greatest importance, however, is his facility for language. It is through language that the child is able to decode a set of symbols into a language with which, we hope, he is familiar. His facility with language will therefore influence his success in decoding, as it will provide meaningful associations for the visual and auditory discrimination involved in learning to read.

Activities designed to encourage skill in both visual and auditory discrimination will be important to the child who is slow to read. Research that has related reading achievement to pre-reading visual discrimination tasks has found a closer association between the two when the discrimination activities used letter-like forms. This supports the notion that training tasks should always be directly related to the basic skill being taught. Auditory sensory organization depends upon good auditory memory and articulation skills. Research in this area supports a phonic approach to reading acquisition and progress.

Most teachers of reading probably use a combination of visual discrimination and auditory discrimination — 'look and say' first and then 'phonics'. It may be that failure to learn to read is because the child's sensory organization does not develop in line with the change of emphasis from visual to phonic methods. If he has visual discrimination difficulties, then he may not benefit from the 'look and say' approach at the time it is being used. Then, when these skills improve, whether through maturation or specific teaching, the class has moved on to 'phonics' and he can no longer use his visual discrimination skill. He may therefore fail to apply any discrimination skills as his development is out of step with the teaching to which he is being exposed. This would suggest that the child should be taught a combination of both approaches. We have found that the emphasis upon letter shape and sound, which is integral to the Goad method for teaching keyboard familiarity (p. 84) has blended well with the less formal approach to reading through total immersion in a reading environment where the teacher is using schemes such as 'paired reading' (McKenzie, 1980; Topping and Wolfendale, 1985).

The child may have poor eye movements, which will be complicated by the fact that he is also trying to scan the page for some letters or words that he can recognize. The integration of writing and reading activities helps the child to recognize words as visual gestalts and also helps to overcome confusion over word orientation. If the child tends to lose his place on the page or has left-to-right directionality difficulties, there is a simple aid, *Line-tracker*, available from LDA. Line-tracker is a transparent plastic pointer that targets both the line and the next word to be read; it looks very 'hi-tec' and therefore older children are happy to use it.

Spelling

It has been said that the school subjects presenting the greatest obstacles to children with a visual–motor difficulty are spelling and number work. Spelling is an *encoding* task. We assume that the child knows what he wants to say and now has to translate the sound of the word into letter combinations. When writing, the child cannot leave out words or parts of words as he might when reading. To encode a word the child has to say it to himself (vocal or sub-vocal articulation demanding motor control). He will then write it and check the feel of it (kinaesthetic memory), the look of it (visual memory) and then read it again (auditory memory). Finally he may check it against familiar rules (reasoning and comprehension).

The ability to spell correctly is, again, associated with the visual discrimination of letter-like rather than non-literal shapes. It is also dependent upon visual sensory organization and on visual memory, which helps the child cope with the irregularities of English spelling. The child also needs good auditory–sensory integration and memory, and motor organization, so that he can articulate and vocalize and build up unfamiliar words.

It is doubtful that the child will be able to cope with a class spelling list. It is more realistic to analyse the child's free writing and select errors that are at least meaningful to him. The teacher may be able to identify patterns of errors and discover whether or not he finds it easier to spell words that look alike (visual memory) or sound alike (auditory memory). A very good programme for teaching spelling is *Catchwords* by Charles Cripps (1983), available from LDA. The word-processing facility on the electric typewriter or the class computer (Chapter 5) is now helping children to draft and redraft work until they get spelling and construction correct. This activity is proving to be a powerful self-motivator and teaching aid.

Number

Difficulties with reading and writing will themselves handicap a child's progress in number; reading more so than writing because teachers are more prepared to give the child the benefit of the doubt when he writes the correct answer but the figures are the wrong way around. However, modern mathematics emphasizes the importance of understanding concepts of quantity and assumes the increased use of concrete materials. The motor impaired child has therefore to carry out operations involving sensory and motor organization. If these are not well developed, he will spend most of his effort on the spatial arrangement of the material and little on understanding its relevance to the task in hand. The teacher needs to be aware of this and may find that the child prefers to depend upon verbal formulations and labelling when using concrete materials in the acquisition of number concepts.

Poor sensory and motor organization may also underlie the child's difficulty in setting out written sums, coping with the arrangement of hundreds, tens and units, and in computation. We add units, tens and hundreds from the right to the left, then name them from the highest value from the left. Digits need to be lined up from the right to allow the place values to correspond vertically, but this conflicts with the left-to-right sequence that the child has learned for working with words. It is often more simple to set out sums for a child. The use of an abacus may be essential for some time.

Auditory attention and memory are important in mental arithmetic. The poor digit memory that has been noted in studies of children with learning difficulties may be a handicap in a wide variety of classroom tasks. Poor visual and auditory memory will make it extremely difficult for a child to hold a particular number in mental computation; it will effect cookery, science and CDT. It could also prevent him from playing a part in class 'jobs', such as counting out the milks or telling the office how many are having lunch.

Training sensory and motor organization

It has been argued that training in sensory and motor organization has in itself little effect upon achievement in specific basic educational attainments. But there is evidence to show that children's performance in those aspects of sensory and motor organization in which they are being specifically trained does improve. It may be that much of the benefit comes from participation in carefully graded activities that enable them to make progress, which is perceived as successful by both child and teacher. The self-fulfilling prophesy then has a 'knock on' effect.

Such a notion suggests that the teacher can best help the child if she pays direct attention to the basic educational attainments themselves and does not waste time with pre-skill activities. However, if the teacher looks carefully at the way in which the child attempts to learn and then analyses just what he can and cannot do, she may well trace the child's problems back to deficiencies in the sensory and motor organization of the task and so find herself teaching visual or auditory discrimination or motor organization skills. The difference will be that the training tasks will be directly related to the basic educational attainments.

Training programmes

The mainstream teacher will have little time to work through a perceptual–motor training programme with an individual child. Chosen activities need to be those a group of children will enjoy doing and also benefit from. *Handbook for Teachers, Perceptual Motor Training* (Wolfendale and Bryans, 1979, 87 update) is a useful booklet, inexpensive and containing not only an observation sheet to help the teacher identify specific areas of weakness but also activities to remediate them.

The authors intend the teacher to build a programme of her own, which will respond to the child's particular difficulties. They say that perceptual–motor difficulties are frequently developmental and that sometimes only a little practice is necessary for observable progress. To carry out the activities the teacher needs no special resources; the paper and pencil activities are easily copied and duplicated. We don't always associate a game of 'I spy' with a child's ability in visual recognition and auditory discrimination, or 'Kim's game' with visual memory. This is why this particular programme is so useful for mainstream work.

An extensive review of research on the perceptual and motor development of children, which examines its implications for the study of learning disabilities and the development of training programmes, can be found in Wedell (1973). The importance of perceptual abilities and reading has been well documented by Tansley (1967), who also outlines a perceptual training programme. Daniels and Diack (1970) provide a battery of diagnostic tests that classroom teachers in schools for children with a physical disability find most useful.

A curriculum-based approach to learning difficulties

As has already been said, a curriculum-based approach to identifying a child's specific learning difficulties will allow them to be described in terms relevant to teacher action and is optimistic in the implication that change is possible. Perceptual difficulties are important theoretically and they do guide the teacher towards suitable training activities. However, they do not, as such, tell the teacher what to teach or how to adapt what she is teaching so that the child can cope more easily with the subject matter.

Two very useful books that take this approach are *Learning Difficulties in Reading and Writing* (Reason and Boote, 1987), and *Classroom Responses to Learning Difficulties* (Reban and Postlethwaite, 1988). The first grew from a collection of ideas that emerged from the authors' own experiences as teachers of children with specific learning difficulties. To these were added those of colleagues, in particular specialist teachers. The teaching methods they offer are not to be seen as an 'infallible prescription' but as suggestions that have proved successful in the past. It is an attempt to assemble enough ideas to enable all teachers, and parents, to give the child some appropriate help. The suggestions have been written with primary schoolchildren in mind but the authors say they could be modified for older pupils.

The second book, *Classroom Responses to Learning Difficulties*, is more relevant to the secondary teacher. Its aim is to help mainstream teachers extend the range of strategies they can use in their own classrooms and to improve the interchange of information between mainstream and special-needs staff. As well as being a useful guide to identifying specific difficulties and providing concrete examples of how to implement the strategies suggested, the book is designed to serve as a basis for INSET in the secondary school and as a text for initial teacher training.

The key to helping a motor impaired child who also has associated learning difficulties within a mainstream class is to accept that he has a reduced capacity for incidental, unstructured learning. It is not enough to provide a stimulating, interesting environment; careful thought must be given to how the child will be able to learn through the classroom experiences on offer. Both the books mentioned above suggest that the teacher should make a careful assessment of what the child already knows and, through such assessment, decide upon the next stage of the teaching–learning process. The teacher then has to take the child forward in stages appropriate to his rate of learning. Teaching targets may need to involve small steps so that the child experiences success and not failure. Skills will need to be taught beyond the point of mastery; they will need to be over-learned. They also need to be generalized and so the more varied the way in which a skill can be practised, the more able the child will be to use that skill in alternative contexts. Additional support will be most effective if it is provided within on-going work in the classroom. Whether or not this is given in withdrawal or in class will depend very much upon the nature of the activity and the child's ability to work without distraction.

If the child has a visual or hearing impairment

Slight hearing loss or defective vision are often associated with a physical impairment. In either case the advice of a teacher who is a specialist in each area will be necessary. The following ideas are included to raise awareness of possible difficulties (some of which have been considered in Chapter 5) and to provide a point of contact when discussing the child with the advisory teacher.

Visual impairment

The arrangement of furniture and his seating position will need to take account of lighting and the siting of electric sockets for any additional aids that may be prescribed. When preparing lesson content, consider the presentation of text and diagrams; often the contrast, print style and spacing can be more important than print size. Foreground and background colour may also affect the child's ability to 'see'.

Teaching method may need to be adapted to enable the child to contribute to and join in lessons. 'Teaching by telephone' is a good way to explain the need to describe materials held up to the class or displayed on a board. Directional instructions also need to be clear and unambiguous — for example, 'on the right' or 'on the window side of the room', rather than 'over there'.

Be aware of safety hazards. The pupil's presence may provide a legitimate reason for enforcing school and classroom rules and for generally considering others. Running in the corridors or chairs not pushed back under tables and desks may create a dangerous environment for the child with poor sight. The teacher also needs to be aware that the child may be unable to recognize different facial expressions and may therefore have no pre-warning of mood or expectations. This could land the child in trouble!

For further information on visual impairment, please see *Partially Sighted Children* (Corley, Robinson and Lockett, 1989), which is another volume in the *Practical Integration in Education* series published by NFER-NELSON.

Hearing impairment

Good vision is very important for children who cannot hear very well. It is also helpful if the child can sit near to the front of the class so that he can see the teacher's face clearly. There needs to be good lighting, without glare.

Many children with hearing loss cope by being able to lip-read but this can be difficult if the teacher is moving about and not looking directly at a child. Shouting, far from being easier to understand, is more difficult because it exaggerates the movements of the mouth.

Beards will obstruct lip-reading — so will talking to the class whilst writing on the board! The teacher should speak with normal rhythm and intonation and try to be at the same horizontal level as the child.

The hearing impaired child will have difficulty in learning new vocabulary and this should be taken into consideration, especially when a new subject is introduced. He will also find it difficult to take notes and lip-read at the same time. The provision of lesson notes would be a great help to him.

The National Library for the Handicapped Child (University of London, Institute of Education) is an excellent resource for any child with a disability, his teacher and his parents. The library holds information on a wide range of conditions as well as books (many with Braille overlays or sign language in the text), audiovisual aids and software.

The Hearing Impaired Child (Goldstein, 1989), provides detailed information for mainstream teachers. A further volume in the *Practical Integration in Education* series, it will help readers to understand the full implications of hearing deficits.

7 Towards Adult Independence

The social life of the school

If the motor impaired child is to be fully integrated into the life of the school, then he has to have the same freedoms as everyone else. School is not just about lessons, it is also the place where most children make their first real friends. It is here that the child learns how to relate to others and his self-image develops as a reflection of how he sees himself in relation to his peers.

Most children also have a full social life outside school. Being free to 'play out', to 'party' or go to the pub is taken for granted by the able-bodied. In order to live with similar freedoms, the child with a motor impairment may have to have the support of his family for transport; each event may need to be carefully timed so that he will not need to visit the toilet; and some events may not be possible because the venues are not accessible to someone in a wheelchair or on crutches.

Before the motor impaired child starts at a mainstream school his ability to be a part of the social life of that school needs to be seriously considered. If changes need to be made, it is more expedient to be prepared for them in advance and so avoid disappointment at a later stage.

Mealtimes

The fact that a child has a restricted diet or needs help with eating should not prevent him from eating with his friends. However, he may need adapted cutlery or non-slip place mats (Chapter 3) and his chair or wheelchair must be at the correct height. With the help of the occupational therapist this can all be sorted out before the child arrives.

Secondary school canteens can prove more of a problem. Nowadays they are usually self-service, and there may be a rail before the counter to control the queue. The child may need someone else to carry his tray or have the use of a trolley. If the rail is too close to the counter, a wheelchair may not get through. Many canteens now have the chairs fixed around the table. These are very difficult for a child with limited mobility and there is no space for wheelchairs. We know of one college that is committed to taking students with physical disabilities, which thoughtfully left one complete table without fitted chairs so that the wheelchairs could fit around it. This created a 'ghetto' effect, as all the disabled students had to sit and eat as a group!

Playtime

All children need to 'play': to be on their own so that they can make relationships in their own time and on their own terms. Very often, the child has
to attend therapy during playtime; if so, then the important time for social
contact is reduced. To get from one lesson to the next is often a major issue
and not a time for the motor impaired child to spend in idle gossip. There
has to be a compromise between educational and medical considerations in
relation to the all-round development of the child. The motor impaired child
may have to stay inside if the weather is bad or because the playground is
too dangerous a place for him to be. Possibly, staff could organize some indoor activities, attractive to a large group of children, so that Christopher is
not the only child who has to 'stay in'. Though why any children should
have to go out to play in polluted city air when they would rather finish
their painting or read a book is another issue.

Clubs and societies

The room that any activity is to be held in needs to be accessible to the
motor impaired child and, as clubs and societies are usually held in the lunch
hours or after school, it would seem a simple thing to choose a suitable
room. A bigger problem is that of transport. It may not be possible for the
child to stay on late at school if the education authority will not pay for or
alter the time of the school bus or the taxi and guide. Unless the child's parents are able to organize private transport, he will be excluded.

School outings

Days out and school journeys provide marvellous opportunities for a motor
impaired child to develop social and independence skills. Being away from
home, maybe for the first time, allows them to be their own person and they
may be able to demonstrate skills and qualities that were not realized at
school. To make the outing a success it is important that either the teacher
or the person who will be responsible for the motor impaired child has a
'trial run' or makes contact with others who have visited before, to ensure
that access is suitable and that the child will be able to manage. Many mu-
seums and galleries now keep wheelchairs on site. This is useful, as the child
may need to rest at some point during the visit. If the school is thinking
about buying a new mini-bus it would be practical to get one with a tail-lift.
Even if the school only has one child who needs to use it, it could be hired

out to groups of disabled or elderly people to recoup the additional cost of fitting the lift.

Making friends

Sometimes the child who has a motor impairment finds it very difficult to know how to make friends. If he is an only child and has had only limited social contacts before coming to school, the teacher may need to construct situations that will encourage him to 'open up'. He could share a practical task with another child who is sensitive and will not dominate him but who is held in high regard by the rest of the class.

There are children with disabilities who have been spoilt at home. Their world may have been dominated by adults and as a result they can be very precocious. They may be in danger of alienating themselves; indeed, sometimes it seems as if they are behaving badly on purpose. They will need help to change this pattern of behaviour before it does too much damage.

If the child has a welfare assistant, the continuous presence of an adult must not act as a barrier to making friends. As the child gets older, he may be slower to mature both physically and emotionally. Children are quick to notice this and may naturally exclude him from certain group activities. This is a difficult one to handle and depends greatly upon the quality of the relationship that was present when they were younger.

Privacy

The child may need to have a degree of privacy for using the toilet or changing for PE. He needs to be able to accept and cope with his condition without being stressed by the curiosity of other children. All children love to gossip, and lurid descriptions of urinary appliances are not going to do much to help the child establish a positive self-image as a normal child who just happens to have a disability.

Planning a leavers' programme

Planning for the future realistically

Many teachers reading this book will be more interested in those issues that relate to physical care, classroom organization and access to the curriculum.

The thought that, one day, little Christopher, Benjamin and Emma will have to take place in the real world might not occur. If it should, then it will not be considered particularly relevant. However, planning for the future of a child with a motor impairment needs to start from infancy. Physical and intellectual growth patterns may not run smoothly and the child's life will be one long fight to keep him as 'normal' as possible. In an effort to do their best for the child, many adults, especially those close to him, will have nurtured unrealistic hopes and ambitions in a natural attempt to encourage interest in an independent future.

All too often, teachers in special education have tried to protect children from negative experiences simply because they feel, quite justifiably, that the child has failed enough without having more failure thrust upon him. A combination of over-protective parents and too many caring adults in the school environment, although this may be necessary for the child's physical independence, is not always conducive to personal independence of thought and understanding. The able-bodied child has the opportunity to 'work through' his unrealistic ambitions in childhood role-plays and attempts to 'test the water' when discussing possible future careers with his friends and his parents. He learns from their reactions and modifies his aspirations accordingly. If the child with a motor impairment does not have these same opportunities, we cannot expect him to develop a realistic view of his own potential. There should be opportunities for the child to explore his ideas and make mistakes whilst he is in a safe and caring environment.

Social skills training

Most young people find the adolescent period difficult to cope with. It is a time when they are trying to become independent of their parents, to develop an identity and a set of personal values. At the same time they are having to cope with physiological changes, emerging sexuality and the problems of future training and employment. For young people coping with both a motor impairment and adolescence, such problems are compounded. If one accepts that the origins of human competence lie in intra-familial relationships and parent–child interaction or in early childhood experiences (the hidden curriculum of the home), then it might be legitimate to assume that the physically impaired child, by the nature of his disability and its effect upon a totally unsuspecting new mother, might start life deprived in one or more areas that may influence his future social competence.

The influence of a motor impairment upon the development of a child's social skill is greater and more direct during adolescence. It is now that physique is most important and bound up with self-concept. The emerging adult has a need for social approval, and yet his condition may mean that he is out of synchrony with his peers and so his need to be perceived as 'the same' may not be satisfied. His peers may recognize subtle differences in his rate of intellectual, physical and social development and comment upon this or outrightly reject him from 'the gang'. The need for sameness, which is demonstrated in the fads and cliques so common amongst teenagers, may exclude the motor impaired child, regardless of a shared environment.

The ability to achieve a natural and easy interaction with non-disabled persons is an important indication of the extent to which the motor impaired child's preferred definition of himself — the fact that he is different physically but not socially — has been accepted. As long as his relationship with his class-mates remains inhibited, as long as he is always on the edge of the group and never the leader, then he has good reason to believe that he is being denied 'normal' status. Like every other child he will have to work for his acceptance, first of all at school and then at college or work. He will need to understand that the world is not full of caring people who will make allowances for his difficulties. If the child is in a wheelchair or on crutches, and so has neither the usual freedom of movement to circulate in social situations nor communicate face to face (unless the other person is sitting down), he will need to develop strategies that allow him to catch and hold the attention of others and make them want to know him for himself.

Social skills training programmes originated from the work of social psychologists who studied the behaviour of people in social situations in order to identify its basic elements and the way they are used in various interactions. There is now a growing body of knowledge about the non-verbal aspects of communication, speech and conversation, as well as of the rules of behaviour that determine the structure of interactions. Today it is possible to buy a range of books on the subject. Usually the concept of social skill is implicit in material that looks more generally at 'life skills' or 'moral education'. Whatever its title, the material is most useful for developing awareness, allowing discussion and encouraging practice in getting on with others.

The *Startline* series (Schools Council, 1978) is the Schools Council Moral Education project for middle school years. The books are short collections of children's own experiences and aim to help pupils to identify those occasions when they can alter the pattern of events by their own initiative and choose thoughtfully from alternative courses of action.

Problem Page (Porter, 1979) presents for discussion many of the common emotional problems facing adolescents. Each problem is shown in a realistic documentary form, using a diary extract, letter, newspaper article or phone conversation that highlights a specific situation. Then a series of graded questions leads the pupils to analyse or discuss and reflect on that situation.

Starting out (Gowar, 1984) is a life-skills record book, which is designed to help the child make realistic decisions about himself and his life. *Skills for Life* (Besley and Byles, 1979) is designed to meet the needs of young people who are about to make or who have just made the transition from school to work. The transition to the world of work throws up countless problems for young people and this programme attempts to bring students into confrontation with all sorts of situations and help them to meet these with equanimity and confidence.

A comprehensive programme with progressive exercises is *Lifeskills Teaching Programmes* (Hopson and Scally, 1982), which both defines what 'lifeskills' are and offers practical suggestions for their development in the classroom. The authors maintain that in the modern world of unemployment and uncertainty, students must learn to cope flexibly with unexpected and rapid changes in a working environment. Students need to be both competent and personally resilient and this programme makes a persuasive case for the inclusion of personal skills development in the curriculum of every secondary school and college.

Examinations, further education and employment

Like all children, those with a motor impairment, however severe, are entitled to leave school at the age of 16 years. But many, including those with minimal impairments, may have missed long periods of formal education through illness and hospitalization. They may also be socially immature and have lacked many of the experiences and opportunities available to able-bodied young people of the same age. The law allows that a young person can stay at school up to their nineteenth birthday if they choose to do so. Many children who are in special education do so, possibly transferring for periods of time to residential training courses, which allow them some time away from their parents and teach them a degree of independence. Of course most youngsters prefer to leave and continue their education at Colleges of Further Education. These colleges are catering more and more for students with a wide range of special needs and many will accept very severely disabled students who come directly to them from special schools.

Preparing for examinations

The motor impaired child in mainstream will be expected to prepare for and complete public examinations in subject areas within his capabilities. The current examination in Great Britain is the GCSE. This entails the completion of on-going course work over a two-year period, which is assessed internally by the school and moderated by external examiners. In addition, the child is still required to sit a traditional examination.

The motor impaired child works slowly; this may be for intellectual reasons or for straightforward physical ones. The amount of course work currently required across all subjects is a daunting prospect for both child and teacher. He will need additional support from the special needs staff in the organization of his study programme so that the best possible use can be made of limited time and physical stamina. For example, it may be possible to enter the same piece of work for two examinations. We know of one boy who linked Design Realization with Graphical Communication and it is possible that there could be similar links within the Humanities.

Children with a physical disability who receive their education in a special school have always been allowed to use a typewriter for their examinations if this was necessary. In mainstream school this issue has only recently been raised and teachers are not familiar with the necessary procedures for permission to be obtained from the examinations boards. In the early days of this break from tradition — all of three years ago — it was known for teachers to reject the idea out of hand and say that it could not possibly be allowed. The cost of employing a separate invigilator for the child whose 'typewriter would make too much noise and disturb the others' was a stumbling block on one occasion! The examination boards also needed some persuading that this facility should be extended to motor impaired children in mainstream.

It is important that those subject teachers who have a motor impaired child in their class should take the time to liaise with the member of staff who coordinates the public examinations so that the appropriate arrangements to satisfy the school's particular examination board can be made. As this may mean contacting the educational psychologist or the child's doctor, plenty of time needs to be allowed. The minimum would be two years in advance, or as soon as the child has chosen his options and is about to start preparing course work. An excellent little book explaining the system and providing addresses and examples of the necessary reports that need to be completed can be obtained from the Diagnostic Centre for Learning Difficulties in London. *Examination Provision for Candidates with Specific Learning Difficulties: GCSE Edition* (Bostock, 1987).

Although it is difficult to accept the teacher's attitude concerning the additional costs of allowing a child to use a typewriter, the point about noise is a valid one. Children coming up to examinations from now on will have been using their typewriters in class from a young age and so it could be argued that their peers will be used to the electronic noises they make. This is an unfair assumption, as when one is under stress the slightest thing can be a distraction. Furthermore, some children with a motor impairment may need to get up during the examination and move around to ease pressure on a part of the body or to relax certain muscles. They may need to go to the lavatory, have a snack, additional drinks, or medication. They will most certainly be eligible for extra time in which to complete the paper. This all needs to be taken into consideration when planning for additional invigilation time.

At CENMACH we are able to loan a back-up typewriter during the examination period if this is requested. This gives the child additional confidence, as machines can break down at the most inopportune moments.

Moving on into further education or training.

When a youngster moves on, either to another school's Sixth Form Centre, or into a Further Education College or a job scheme, it is especially important that all the information that has been collected concerning his physical and intellectual abilities and difficulties should go with him. Ideally he will be able to visit his new environment with the teacher who is responsible for his pastoral care, meet the staff, check out access and understand the demands that are going to be made upon him. Good communication prior to entrance will be crucial for success on the first day of the new term or the work placement.

The careers service

Careers officers offer the first link between school and the outside worlds. All local authorities are required to maintain a careers service to provide vocational guidance for young people in full- or part-time education. The service links with the employment service, which is available when students leave school or complete their studies. Most careers services now have specialist officers to work with students who have disabilities. These are highly skilled in this area and are realists when it comes to deciding what is the most appropriate way forward for a child who is motor impaired. It is important that the teacher responsible for 'careers' in the mainstream secondary school knows of their existence and calls upon them for advice. It is a fact that the children who leave special schools usually have more successful after-school placements, be they in education, training or open employment, than does the minimally handicapped youngster who has been thrown into the real world without realistic thought being given to his abilities and needs.

Grants and allowances

The young adult needs also to understand just what his rights are to grants and allowances that relate directly to his disability. This should be a subject covered either by the specialist careers officer or by a member of staff at his school as part of the social skills' curriculum or leavers' programme. A useful publication that comes out annually is the *Disability Rights Handbook* (Disability Alliance, each April), which devotes three sections to children with disabilities and explains educational grants and extra allowances. For the year 1988–89, students were eligible for an additional grant over and above their mandatory award. The sum of £730 can be spent on additional costs (other than travel costs) incurred because of the disability. It is up to the local authority to decide whether the particular cost is necessarily incurred but, in the past, they have been known to honour claims for typewriters, computers, extra heating and dietary needs, and help with readers, amanuenses and other paid helpers and extra aids. Travel expenses, which may be considerable, should be included in the calculation of the mandatory award. If the student has a discretionary award, additional finance for aids or travel is not obligatory but many local authorities will pay these costs.

The Snowden Award Scheme provides bursaries of up to £1000 to students with disabilities who are undertaking some form of further education or training. In the past the scheme has helped students with course fees, equipment and wheelchairs.

'Skill', the National Bureau for Students with Disabilities, publishes a regular newsletter and is able to provide information and support to young people with special needs. They take care to keep up to date with any legislation that may affect a student with a disability, and they organize conferences and advertise relevant courses.

Going to work

If a youngster is determined to go out to work without any further education or training, then it is important that he has some experience of a real work situation whilst he is still at school. The initial search for a job may confront him, for the first time, with the real limitations of his disability and the attitudes of the able-bodied towards it and therefore, indirectly, with himself.

The disablement resettlement officer (DRO) is a specially trained member of the Employment Service Agency staff. He works both with the employers and with the disabled person in an effort to find jobs that will offer useful and appropriate work. He will then keep in touch with the young person to ensure that all is going well. Again, it is important that the motor impaired school-leaver does not miss out on such advice and support just because he is in a mainstream school. Being able to cope with a day at school where there are caring people and where allowances have been made for physical and intellectual limitations does not mean to say that the teenager will be able to cope with an eight-hour day, no frequent breaks, possibly no opportunity to sit down, plus having to relate to a new set of people who may 'take the mickey'.

The Disabled Person's (Employment) Act of 1944 (HMSO, Revised 1958) initiated a register of disabled people. This is kept by the Employment Services Agency and at careers offices. A person does not have to register and many prefer not to, but to do so does have certain advantages and these should be weighed up by the youngster and his family with the advice of the careers officer. For example, although a motor impaired school leaver who was intending to go out and find a job could contact the DRO for advice, he would not normally receive the special facilities offered, such as help with finding a job or help with travel costs, unless he was registered. Registration can last for one to ten years and is applicable to those who are 'substantially handicapped in obtaining or keeping employment'.

Readers may wish to refer to a Classified List of Principal Acts of Parliament Affecting Disabled People (pub. RADAR). Price £1.20.

Significant living without paid employment

Paid employment usually provides a youngster with a sense of purpose and social status. Unfortunately, many children with a motor impairment are going to face life without employment. In addition, they may be deprived of the freedom of social movement taken for granted by their peers. Many look forward to a life at home in front of the television with the odd outing when someone is free to accompany them. Much will depend upon how they have been prepared for the real world, and being educated in a mainstream school is a first step in that direction. However, emphasis upon an academic curriculum could overlook the fact that these children, more than any, need to be able to use their leisure time constructively. Hobbies and interests encouraged at school will possibly be of more lasting value than educational qualifications.

8 Planning for Successful Integration — The Social and Psychological Implications

It is very easy to emphasize the practical and educational issues surrounding the full integration of a motor impaired child into mainstream school and to fail to take account of what the child feels about it all. Teachers and parents, in a genuine attempt to give the child the benefits of a mainstream curriculum, can overlook the psychological trauma they may be causing the child. The child, fearful of seeming ungrateful and wanting to be just like the rest of the kids in the street, makes the best of his situation. Mainstreaming is still in its infancy; it will be interesting to hear what the children have to say about their experiences when they become adults — maybe they would have preferred special education. The true stories of Christopher and Benjamin may help to illustrate the importance of adult awareness of unspoken fears and apprehensions.

Christopher

Christopher started his education in the nursery of a school for children with a physical handicap. By the time he was seven it was very obvious that he was of above average intelligence and fast becoming the class 'clown'. He needed to be stretched academically and socially, and as there was a suitable primary school just across the street, the special school staff began to plan his integration programme.

Chris has cerebral palsy. At this time he was unsteady on his feet, he dribbled and his speech was difficult to understand. Hand coordination was poor and he needed to use a typewriter for all his written work. He was a nervous lad, prone to sweating at the nape of the neck if he had to make a decision such as choosing his lunch. An only child, he had always had the undivided attention of his parents, but one could not say that he was spoilt.

It was not until Chris was ten years old that his programme got under way. The paramedical staff felt that he lacked the confidence necessary to cope with his degree of handicap in a mainstream setting. At this point in time (1978), integration was a new concept and we had no examples to follow. After a successful school journey, the first time away from home, we felt that he was ready to give it a try.

Christopher was due to start in the September term and so, during the summer term, we organized two-way visits between the two schools, shared social events, and the staff of both schools talked and planned. On the first day of the autumn term his typewriter was in place, his special plate, cutlery and cup in the school kitchen, and Chris plus his support teacher arrived in the mainstream class. It was soon apparent that Chris was more able than most of the class; he also had a ready cockney wit, which the children loved. After a couple of days the support teacher withdrew and worked with some of the less able children whilst Chris worked with the teacher and the bulk of the class. We began to notice small but significant changes in him. He tried to control his walk by putting his hands in his pockets; he abandoned the special plate and cup and tried hard to control his dribble and speak more slowly and clearly. His best friend was the class football star, a very high status member of the group, who introduced Chris to real football. By half-term the special school staff began to look for a suitable secondary school placement.

His mother was thrilled. She had invested so much time and energy in encouraging his interests in books and music. She was aware that people stared at him in the street and was gratified by his acceptance in a 'normal' school, which confirmed what she had known all along, that despite his handicap he was no different to any other child. We had a few difficulties. Chris got very tired by the end of the day and on the walk to the library he was always the last, but not alone — someone always stayed behind to keep him company. He still came to school on the school bus, and his special-school friends found it difficult to accept that he should go to a different school. To help him keep in touch we allowed him to stay to 'club' in the special school once a week. In order to fit in his therapy and school transport he had to leave school early and that meant that he usually missed the serialized story at the end of the day.

Just after half-term he was off school for a week with a virus infection. When he returned to school the support teacher was spending part of each day visiting secondary schools on his behalf. One morning Chris got off the school bus and flatly refused to go to the mainstream school. This happened one or two times but each time we managed to persuade him to stick at it. His mother was aware of the difficulty and did not want him to give up. Things got worse and eventually Chris rejoined his class in the special school.

The children in his mainstream class and the staff of both schools were devastated. If Chris could not cope, how could we expect any of the other children to make it in a mainstream setting? His mainstream friends came to see him and begged him to go back to school with them. He refused and would not talk about it to anyone.

In January he told us that 'he just didn't feel comfortable over there'. The school wanted to continue with an integration programme and so it was necessary to try and find out where things had gone wrong. We turned to the educational psychologist's report, completed that autumn. She wrote:

> Personality testing suggests that whilst he is both socially skilful and has a deft sense of humour, his present uncertainties are not surprisingly, stressful to him ... He enjoys [the mainstream school] 'nine out of ten' as he put it, and was proud when he read in assembly.

However, the impression is of a boy who may have to push himself and who may find school quite a strain at times.

Further testing suggested that Christopher is enjoying the extra stimulation afforded by the new opportunities before him, and that he is a child who welcomes such experience. He does, however, also need a sympathetic and understanding adult around for reassurance. He needs to know clearly what is going to happen to him in his future schooling.

We began to ask ourselves how much integration on an individual basis works. Would Chris have been happier if he had had some of his special school friends with him? Gingras *et al.* (1964) point out that upon entering 'normal' school, the handicapped child has to take the responsibility for his own adjustment, to establish new relationships with adults, and to ward off possible verbal attacks and secure the acceptance of his class-mates. At this stage, the child's image of himself, his self-concept, especially that related to attitudes and experiences involving the body, his body, is likely to be intensified as he is now able to compare himself with his non-handicapped peers. If he tries to aspire to the 'normal' in performance, he will expose himself to inferiority and failure. Anderson (1973) says that often a cheerful, outwardly well-adjusted, social child can suffer from strong hidden anxieties.

Davies (1961) says that a social relationship between a person with a visible handicap and an able-bodied person passes through various stages before it becomes normal. Western manners dictate that we do not comment upon any aspect of a person's behaviour or appearance that we perceive as being different to that of ourselves. Chris was accorded, and had to play along with, this 'fictional acceptance' because he knew that it was the only basis upon which he could develop the contact into something more genuine. He was then able to 'develop and project strategies' that allowed the class to identify with him in terms other than those normally associated with imputations of deviance. Chris showed himself to be superior as a comic and a wit, and gifted academically. He stayed close to the football star, a highly presentable companion. In Goffman's (1968) terms he 'covered' very well. He strived to overcome the stereotype of 'handicap', to conceal it and appear as normal as possible.

Now Chris had to sustain this relationship in the face of the many small practical and social problems that began to arise: the fact that he needed help and was always last on the walk to the library; that he was never going to be 'ace' at football; together with the realization that, once serious practice got under way, he was not included, being more hindrance than help. It was very difficult for him to try to be 'normal' whilst at the same time having to admit to certain incidental incapacities, limitations and needs. He may have been afraid that he was accepted out of pity. It may be if there had been other children with similar disabilities in the school, he would have felt more at ease; he would have been amongst his 'own' (Goffman, 1968).

Changing the integration model

We felt that we had failed Christopher in not taking into account his emotional reactions to his situation. Because all seemed to be running smoothly, we had seen no need to draw attention to the details of his condition or its implications for his ability to cope in mainstream. Of course, the teachers were aware but we had not thought to construct a situation whereby Christopher could share this with his friends.

Chris had to face up to the fact that he was physically and functionally different from the other children. Perhaps for the first time in his life he saw clearly the contrast between his functional capabilities and those of his friends. Fishman and Fishman (1971) describe a three-part process — a series of confrontations between the child and his disability through which he has to pass whilst adjusting to it. First of all he wants to understand his difficulty, its causes and its prognosis. Then he wants to express his feelings about it, his anger and his sorrow. These are difficult emotions, which he may be afraid to express, even to those closest to him, his parents. Eventually, if his handicap is to be incorporated into his social identity without stigma, if it is going to be publically acknowledged and accepted, he has to be able to talk about it with his peers.

If we had been aware at the time that such a process of self-acceptance and confrontation was necessary, we would have encouraged a degree of openness to the totality of his problem. We would not have been content with the fact that his seeming no different from the other children meant that the programme had worked. We had paid lip-service to the more progressive attitudes towards disability that were then fashionable. True and successful integration was going to have to acknowledge a child's differences in the fullest sense of the word if this process of confrontation was going to be opened up.

The special-school integration initiative then took on a different form. Two groups of children from the special school were matched for age with two classes in the mainstream school. Through teacher cooperation of the highest quality and the goodwill of paramedical and care staff, with school transport, and backed up by the inspectorate and the administrators in the local education office, we were able to organize integration on both sites. At times it was hectic, with children and staff coming and going, but it worked and it was fun. Integrated activities were organized around the creative arts so that each child could work at his own level. Time for chatting and building relationships was inherent to sharing and acting upon ideas. There were no contrived 'play' situations, which can fail so miserably.

Very soon after the start of the programme one child in particular stood out as someone who could and who wanted to be part of mainstream life. He, too, had cerebral palsy, was unsteady on his feet, dribbled terribly and had very indistinct speech. Benjamin decided to integrate himself into the ordinary school.

Benjamin

Benjamin was more physically impaired than Chris but staff suspected that he was also more intellectually able. An out-going and very determined child, he did not show any anxiety as Chris had done when asked to make independent decisions. We realized just how comfortable Ben was in a different class when he complained at having to leave early to catch the school bus. Gradually he managed to have arrangements made so that he could stay for the full afternoon and, later on, a full day. Within a term he was in the mainstream school for a full week at a time and resenting coming back to the special school for therapy or to catch the bus. The group integration project continued and, although Ben greeted his friends when they visited, he attached himself more and more to the mainstream children and their teacher.

Arrangements were then made for him to attend the mainstream school for his final year at primary level. To do this the mainstream school accepted his younger brother so that his mother could take both children to school at the same time and Ben would not need to use school transport. At the same time a member of care staff was 'seconded' to work in the mainstream school with the groups when they visited and with another, younger child, who we felt would benefit from a full-time placement.

Ben's secondary school was chosen from the results of our survey of schools made in preparation for Christopher's transfer at 11 years of age. We suggested that Ben and his parents look at an all-boys comprehensive church school not too far from their home. Both Ben and his parents were very happy with this choice and the school took pains to find out about his special needs and responded in a positive way to the need for classrooms on the ground floor and his need to use a typewriter in class. By now it was becoming evident that he had a quite extraordinary talent for mathematics and computer science, although his spelling was not up to the same standard.

Ben spent two years at his inner-city mainstream secondary school. The staff were very accommodating: they took time to meet and discuss his progress with both therapists and staff from the special school, and allowed him an individualized timetable so that he could take public examinations in mathematics and computer studies in his second year. An individual support teacher was appointed to stretch him in those subjects where he showed particular ability.

Life was not without its problems. He managed to drop and break two typewriters and lose another. Some staff needed to be encouraged to treat him as they would any other boy. It was pointed out that he was only entitled to one twenty-fifth of any teacher's time and that, just because he had a disability and was extremely bright, he was being allowed to demand more attention from them than was good for him. Staff from the CDT department visited the special school so that they could get ideas for equipment that would allow him to work without damaging himself or the other children, and the physiotherapists advised on suitable games and PE activities. His poor articulation was still a major problem and he refused to carry a small communication aid that would have allowed him to print out short messages or words when others could not understand him. He compromised eventually and used the small VDU on the Typestar to ask and answer questions in class.

Well into his second year, on his own initiative, Benjamin applied for and won a scholarship to one of England's top public schools. He is there now. He acknowledges that it is hard work; the teachers quite rightly make no exceptions for him. He has chosen this style of education for himself and has won it on his own merit — now he has to live with the reality of it. He feels that the long-term benefits are worth the day-to-day problems of walking long distances between lessons with his typewriters and books in a shopping cart, having to dress in a formal uniform and getting up at six in the morning to finish his homework. The school have provided him with an Apple Macintosh microcomputer so that he can access a wide range of mathematical and scientific software, and this he keeps in his room. For classwork he uses the Canon Typestar, supplemented by a Brother BP30 for mathematics.

Benjamin got where he is today because he wanted to get there. He had help along the way but only that which any child would have received had they decided to take the same initiatives. Yuker *et al.* (1960) wrote:

> A disabled person's attitude towards himself and his own self acceptance are not necessarily directly proportional to the extent of his disability. The individual attitudes held by a disabled child towards himself will greatly influence his behaviour.

Perhaps if we had waited until he was older, Christopher would have been able to manage a mainstream secondary curriculum. Perhaps if he had had the opportunity to attend mainstream school from the start as many children do nowadays, he could have coped. There are so many imponderables surrounding the integration issue that we need time and the benefit of hindsight before we can say with confidence what type of school placement is best for any one child. Christopher left the special school at 16 years of age and went to college. He is now taking his 'A' Levels — a confident young man with a fashionable hair style and a girlfriend. He, too, chose what was best for him at a certain time in his life.

Appendix I
List of Addresses

1. Arthritis Care, 6 Grosvenor Crescent, London SW1X 7ER. Tel: 01 235 0902.
2. Association of Swimming Therapy. Secretary: Ted Gowan. 4 Oak Street, Shrewsbury, Shopshire, SY3 7RH. Tel: 0743 4393.
3. Association for Research into Restricted Growth, c/o Pamela Rutt, 24 Pinchfield, Maple Cross, Rickmansworth, Hertfordshire, WD3 2TP. Tel: 0923 770759.
4. Association for Spina Bifida and Hydrocephalus (ASBAH), 22 Upper Woburn Place, London WC1H 0EP. Tel: 01 388 1382.
5. Association of all Speech Impaired Children (AFASIC), 347 Central Markets, Smithfield, London EC1 9NH. Tel: 01 236 3632.
6. Asthma Research Council, St. Thomas' Hospital, Lambeth Palace Road, London SE1 7EH. Tel: 01 928 3099.
7. Blissymbolics Communication Resource Centre (UK), c/o The Spastics Society, 382–384 Newport Road, Cardiff, CF3 7UA. Tel: 0222 496240.
8. Bobath Centre for Physically Handicapped Children, 5 Netherall Gardens, London NW3 5RN. Tel: 01 794 6084.
9. British Association of Teachers of the Deaf (BATOD), The Rycroft Centre, Royal Schools for the Deaf, Stanley Road, Cheadle Hulme, Cheadle, Cheshire SK8 6RK. Tel: 061 437 5951.
10. British Diabetic Association, 10 Queen Anne Street, London W1M 0BD. Tel: 01 323 1531.
11. British Epilepsy Association, Crowthorne House, New Wokingham Road, Wokingham, Berkshire RG11 3AY. Tel: 0344 773122.
12. British Heart Foundation, 102 Gloucester Place, London W1H 4DH. Tel: 01 935 0185.
13. British Sports Association for the Disabled, Stoke Mandeville Stadium, Harvey Road, Aylesbury, Bucks HP21 8PP. Tel: 0296 84848.
14. Brittle Bones Society, 112 City Road, Dundee DO2 2PW. Tel: 0382 67603
15. Canon (UK) Ltd. (Personal Products Division), Canon House, Manor Road, Wallington, Surrey SM6 0AJ. Tel: 01 733 3173.
16. Canon (UK) Ltd. (Service Centre), Gatwick Road, Crawley, West Sussex RH10 2HF. Tel: 0293 518899.
17. Centre for Motor and Associated Communication Handicap (CENMACH), Charlton Park School, Charlton Park Road, London SE7 8HX. Tel: 01 316 7589.
18. College of Speech Therapists, Harold Poster House, 6 Lechmere Road, London NW2 5BU. Tel: 01 459 8521.
19. Communication Aids Centre (*see* the Wolfson Centre).
20. Department of Health, Alexander Fleming House, Elephant and Castle, London SE1 6BY. Tel: 01 407 5522.
21. Devilbiss Co. Ltd., Ringwood Road, Northbourne, Bournemouth, Dorset, BH11 9LH. Tel: 0202 571111.
22. Diagnostic Centre for Learning Difficulties, Ebury Street, London SW1. Tel: 01 821 8011.
23. Disability Alliance, 25 Denmark Street, London WC2 8NJ. Tel: 01 240 0806.
24. Disability Unit, Department of Transport, 2 Marsham Street, London SW1P 3EB. Tel: 01 212 5257/3547.
25. Disabled Living Foundation, 380–384 Harrow Road, London W9 2HU. Tel: 01 289 6111.
26. Disabled Photographers Society, c/o Scrase, 151 Sandy Lane South, Wallington, Surrey. SM6 9NP. Tel: 01 647 3179.
27. Disfigurement Guidance Centre, Clydesdale Bank Buildings, High Street, Newburgh, Fife, KY15 5HF, Scotland.
28. Easiaids Ltd. 48 Mill Green Road, Mitcham, Surrey CR4 4HY. Tel: 01 648 4186.
29. Fashion Service for the Disabled, 010–030 Saltaire Workshop, Ashley Lane, Shipley, West Yorkshire BD17 5JS. Tel: 0274 597487.

30. Foundation for the Communication for the Disabled, Foundation House, Church Street West, Woking, GU2P 1DJ. Tel: 04862 27848.
31. Friedreich's Ataxia Group, Burleigh Lodge, Knowle Lane, Cranleigh, Surrey GU6 8RD. Tel: 0483 272741.
32. Taxi Card Scheme (contact your local Social Services Office).
33. GLC Supplies, Mill Mead road, Ferry Lane, Tottenham, N17 9NQ. Tel: 01 801 3333.
34. Headway, National Head Injuries Association, 200 Mansfield Road, Nottingham NG1 3HX. Tel: 0602 622 382.
35. Hellerman Co., Hellerman House, Harris Way, Windmill Road, Sunbury on Thames TW16 7EW. Tel: 0932 781 888/9.
36. Hestair Hope Education, [Rehabilitation Equipment], St. Philips Drive, Royton, Oldham OL2 6AG. Tel: 061 633 6611.
37. Inner London Educational Computing Centre (ILECC), John Ruskin Street, London SE5 0PQ. Tel: 01 735 9123.
38. International Cerebral Palsy Society, 5a Netherall Gardens, London NW3 5RN. Tel: 01 794 9761.
39. Joncare. 7 Ashville Trading Estate, Nuffield Way, Abingdon, Oxford DX14 1RL. Tel: 0235 28120.
40. LDA, Duke Street, Wisbech, Cambs PE13 2AE. Tel: 0945 63441.
41. Lefties, Dept. D1, PO Box 52, South DO Manchester M20 8JP. Tel: 061 445 0159.
42. Living and Learning (see LDA).
43. F. Llewellyn and Co Ltd., Carlton Works, Carlton Street, Liverpool L3 7ED. Tel: 051 236 5311.
44. Mobilia Systems, Drake House, 18 Creekside, London SE8 3DZ. Tel: 01 692 7141.
45. Mobility Information Service, Copthorne Community Hall, Shelton Road, Shrewsbury SY3 8TD. Tel: 0743 68383.
46. Muscular Dystrophy Group of Great Britain, Nattrass House, 35 Macauley Road, London SW4 0QP. Tel: 01 720 8055.
47. National Deaf Children's Society, 45 Hereford Road, London W2 5AH. Tel: 01 229 9272.
48. Nottingham Rehab, Ludlow Hill Road, West Bridgford, Nottingham NG2 6HD. Tel: 0602 234251.
49. Ortho-Kinetics (UK) Ltd. (Care Chair Division), Wednesfield, Wolverhampton WV13 3XA. Tel: 0902 866166.
50. Parents in Partnership, 25 Woodnook Road, London SW16 6TZ.
51. Partially Sighted Society, 40 Wordsworth Street, Hove, East Sussex BN3 5BH. Tel: 0273 736053.
52. Philip and Tacey, North Way, Andover, Hants SP10 5BA. Tel: 0264 332171.
53. REMAP (Rehabilitation Engineering Movement Advisory Panels), 25 Mortimer Street, London W1N 8AB. Tel: 01 637 1266.
54. RML (Research Machines Ltd.), PO Box 75, Oxford OX2 0BW. Tel: 0865 791234.
55. Rompa, PO Box 5, Wheatbridge Road, Chesterfield, Derby S40 2AE. Tel: 0246 211777.
56. Royal Association for Disability and Rehabilitation (RADAR), 25 Mortimer Street, London W1N 8AB. Tel: 01 637 5400.
57. Royal National Institute for the Blind (Peterborough), Production and Distribution Centre, Bakewell Road, Orton Southgate, Peterborough PE2 0XU. Tel: 0733 370 777.
58. Royal Society for the Prevention of Accidents (ROSPA), Cannon House, Priory Queensway, Birmingham B4 6BS. Tel: 021 233 2461.
59. Scottish Council for Spastics, Rhuemore, 22 Corstorphine Road, Edinburgh EH12 6HP. Tel: 031 337 9876.
60. SHAPE (London), 1 Thorpe Close, London W10 5XL. Tel: 01 960 9245.
61. SKILL (The National Bureau for Students with Disabilities), 336 Brixton Road, London SW9 7AA. Tel: 01 274 0565.
62. Snowden Award Scheme, c/o Vincent House, North Parade, Horsham, W. Sussex RH12 2DA. Tel: 0403 210406.
63. Spastics Society, 12 Park Crescent, London W1N 4EQ Tel: 01 636 5020.
64. Special Access Systems, 4 Benson Road, Oxford OX2 6QH. Tel: 0865 56154.

65. Spinal Injuries Association, Yeoman House, 76 St. James Lane, London N10 3DF. Tel: 01 444 2121.
66. D. A. Thomas (London) Ltd., Architectural Ironmongers, 124/126 Denmark Hill, London SE5 8RX. Tel: 01 733 2101.
67. Tri-Aid Manufacturing Ltd., 32 Welbeck Road, Darnley Industrial Estate, Glasgow G53 7SD. Tel: 041 881 2273.
68. University of London, Institute of Education, 20 Bedford Way, London WC1 0AL. Tel: 01 636 1500, ext. 599 or 01 255 1363.
69. Wolfson Centre, Mecklenburgh Square, London WC1N 2AP. Tel: 01 837 7618.

Appendix II
Reading List

1. ACE (1988). *Special Education Handbook*. London: ACE.
   (This is the third edition of a comprehensive handbook containing information on the 1988 Education Reform Act which has so substantially added to the law on special education. The handbook includes a commentary on all the relevant legislation, both new and old and offers advice at each stage of the special education procedure. ACE is at 18 Victoria Park Square, London E2 9PB.)
2. BAKER, D. and BOVAIR, K. (1989). *Making the Special School Ordinary?* Lewes: Falmer.
3. BEDFORD, S. and ALSTON, J. (1987). *Helping Clumsy Children with Handwriting. A Multi-disciplinary Viewpoint*. Stafford: NARE.
4. BINES, H. (1986). *Redefining Remedial Education*. London, Croom Helm.
5. BOND, T. (1986). *Games for Life and Social Skills*. London: Hutchinson.
6. BOOKIS, J. (1983). *Beyond the School Gate*. London: RADAR.
7. BOSTOCK, A. (1988). *Eyes: Children with Impaired Vision*. London: DCLD.
   (from Ebury Teachers Centre, Sutherland Street, SW18 4HH.)
8. BRANDES, D. and PHILIPS, H. (1977). *Gamsters Handbook*. London: Hutchinson.
9. BRITISH GAS (updated yearly). *Advice for disabled people*. Home Services, 709 Old Kent Road, London SE15 1JJ. Tel: 01 639 2030.
10. CLARK, M. (1988). *Teaching Left Handed Children*. London: Hodder and Stoughton.
11. CORLEY, G., ROBINSON, D. and LOCKETT, S. (1989). *Partially Sighted Children*. Windsor: NFER-NELSON.
12. DESSENT, T. (1987). *Making the Ordinary School Special*. Lewes: Falmer.
13. ELECTRICITY COUNCIL (updated regularly). *Making Life Easier for Disabled People*. The Electricity Council, 30 Millbank, London SW1P 4RD. Tel: 01 834 2333, or contact your local Electricity Board.
14. FAMILY FUND (1988). *After 16, What Next?* York: Family Fund. (available from the Fund at PO Box 50, York YO1 1UY.)
15. FISHMAN, I. (1987). *Electronic Communication Aids: Selection and Use*. London: Taylor and Francis Ltd.
16. GEORGE, S.J. and HART, B. (1983). *Physical Education for Handicapped Children*. London: Souvenir Press.
17. GOLDSTEIN, D. (1989). *The Hearing Impaired Child*. Windsor: NFER-NELSON.
18. GREAT BRITAIN, DEPARTMENT of EDUCATION and SCIENCE (1971). *Physical Education for the Physically Handicapped*. London: HMSO.
19. HALE, G. (1979). *The Source Book for the Disabled*. London: Paddington Press.
20. MILLARD, D. (1984). *Daily Living with a Handicapped Child*. London: Croom Helm.
21. PENSO, D. (1987). *Occupational Therapy for Children with a Disability*. Andover: Thompson Publishing.
22. PETER, M. and BARNES, R. (1982). *Signs, Symbols and Schools. An Introduction to the Use of Non-vocal Communication Systems and Sign Language in Schools*. Stratford-upon-Avon: NCSE.
   (available from 1 Wood Street, Stratford-upon-Avon CV37 6SE.)
23. PETERS, M.L. (1985). *Spelling taught or caught: A New Look*. London: Routledge and Keegan Paul.
24. RAMSDEN, D. THOMPSON, M. (1986). 'Special needs and the GCSE', *British Journal of Special Education*, 13, 4, p. 138–40.
25. SIMMONS, S. (1988). *Examination Arrangements for Students with a Disability*. London: Skill.
   (see List of Addresses.)
26. SPENCE, S. (1983). *Social Skills Training with Children and Adolescents*. Windsor: NFER-NELSON.
27. WEBSTER, A. and ELLWOOD, J. (1985). *The Hearing Impaired child in the Ordinary School*. London: Croom Helm.
28. WEBSTER, A. and McCONNELL, C. (1987). *Children with Speech and Language Difficulties*. London: Cassell Education.

References

AGNEW, N. and POVEY, R. (1984). 'Chess for the physically handicapped', *Special Education, Forward Trends*, 11, 3, 37.

ALSTON, J. and TAYLOR, J. (1985). *The Handwriting File*. Wisbech: LDA.

ALSTON, J. and TAYLOR, J. (1987). *Handwriting. Theory, Research and Practice*. London: Croom Helm.

ALSTON, J. and TAYLOR, J. (1985). *Helping Left Handed Children with Handwriting*, Supplement to *The Handwriting File*. Wisbech: LDA.

ANDERSON, E. (1973). *The Disabled Schoolchild*. London: Methuen.

ASSOCIATION OF SWIMMING THERAPY. (1981). *Swimming for the Disabled*. London: A. and C. Black.

BAILEY, P. (1973). *They can make Music*. Oxford: Oxford University Press.

BATE, M., SMITH, M. and JAMES, J. (1981). *Review of Tests and Assessments in Early Education*. Windsor: NFER-NELSON.

BENDER, L. (1938). *Visual Motor Gestalt Test and Its Clinical Uses*. New York: American Orthopsychiatric Association.

BESLEY, L.K. and BYLES, D. (1979). *Skills for Life*. Cheltenham: Stanley Thornes Ltd.

BOSTOCK A. (1987). *Examination Provision for Candidates with Specific Learning Difficulties: GCSE Edition*. London: DCLD.

BROWN, A. (1987). *Active Games for Children with Movement Problems*. London: Harper and Row.

BUMPHREY, E.E. (1981). *Dressmaking for the Disabled*. London: C.O.T. for Disabled Living Foundation.

CORLEY, G., ROBINSON, D. and LOCKETT, S. (1989). *Partially Sighted Children*. Windsor: NFER-NELSON.

DANIELS, J.C. and DIACK, H. (1970). *The Standard Reading Tests*. London: Chatto and Windus.

DAVIS, F. (1961). 'Deviance disavowal: The management of strained interaction by the visibly handicapped', *Social Problems*, 9, 120–32.

DISABILITY ALLIANCE (annual publication). *Disability Rights Handbook*. London: Disability Alliance.

DISABLED LIVING FOUNDATION (1976). *Kitchen Sense for Disabled or Elderly People*. Oxford: Heinemann Medical.

DUFFY, J. (1974). *Type It*. Bath: 'Better Books'.

FISH, J. (1985). *Educational Opportunities for All?* London: ILEA.

FISHMAN, A. and FISHMAN, D.B. (1971). 'Emotional, cognitive and interpersonal confrontations amongst children with birth defects', *Child Psychiatry and Human Development*, 2, 92–101.

GINGRAS, G., MONGEAU, M., MOREAULT, P., DUPOIS, M., HERBER, B. and CORRIVEAU, C. (1964). 'Congenital abnormalities of the limbs. Psychological and educational aspects'. *Canadian Medical Association Journal*, 91, 15–19.

GOFFMAN, E. (1968). *Stigma. Notes on the Management of a Spoiled Identity*. London: Penguin.

GOLDSTEIN, D. (1989). *The Hearing Impaired Child*. Windsor: NFER-NELSON.

GOWAR, M. (1984). *Starting Out*. London: Collins Educational.

GREAT BRITAIN. DEPARTMENT OF EDUCATION AND SCIENCE (1981). *Education Act*. London: HMSO.

GREAT BRITAIN. DEPARTMENT OF EDUCATION AND SCIENCE. *Assessment and Statement of Special Educational Need*, Circular 1/83. London: HMSO.

GREAT BRITAIN. DEPARTMENT OF EDUCATION AND SCIENCE (1984a). *Access for Disabled Students to Educational Buildings*, Design Note 18. London: DES.

GREAT BRITAIN. DEPARTMENT OF EDUCATION AND SCIENCE (1984b). *Designing for Children with Special Educational Needs in the Ordinary School*, Building Bulletin 61. London: HMSO.

GREAT BRITAIN. DEPARTMENT OF EDUCATION AND SCIENCE (1987). *The National Curriculum, 5–16, a Consultation Document*. London: DES.

GREAT BRITAIN. MINISTRY OF EDUCATION (1944). *Education Act*, section 8 (2). London: HMSO.

GREAT BRITAIN. MINISTRY OF EDUCATION (1954). *Circular 276* (June 25th). London: HMSO.

HANCOCK, J. and ALSTON, J. (1986). 'Handwriting skills in children with spina bifida: assessment, monitoring and measurement'. *British Journal of Special Education*, 13, 155–158.

HOPSON, B. and SCALLY, M. (1982). *Lifeskills Teaching Programme*. Leeds: Lifeskills Associates.

JARMAN, C. *(1977)*. 'A helping hand for slow learners'. *Special Education, Forward Trends*. 4, 4.

JARMAN, C. (1982). *The Development of Handwriting Skills*. Oxford: Blackwell.

JONES, A. (1983). *Science for Handicapped Children*. Human Horizons Series. London: Souvenir Press.

KEMPTHORNE, J. (1978). 'Typewriting Exercises for one-handed People'. St. Albans: St Albans College Library.

KENT COUNTY COUNCIL. EDUCATION DEPARTMENT. (1986). *Physical Education for Children with Special Educational Needs in Mainstream*. Kent: KCC.

McKENZIE, M. (1980). *Helping your Child with Reading: A Parents' Guide*. London: Franklin Watts.

MALE, J. and WARD, J. (1987). *Working Together Towards Independence: Guidelines for Non-teaching Assistants Working with Children with a Physical Disability*. London: RADAR.

MANDELSTAM, D. (1989). *Understanding Incontinence*. London: Chapman and Hall. (Available from the Disabled Living Foundation.)

NEWTON, M. and THOMSON, M. (1982). *The Aston Index. A Classroom Test for Screening and Diagnosis of Language Difficulties*. Wisbech: Living and Learning.

NOLAN, C. (1987). *Under the Eye of the Clock*. London: Weidenfeld and Nicholson.

PETERS, M.L. and CRIPPS, C. (1978). *Catchwords*. Sydney (and London): Harcourt Brace Jovanovich.

PLOWDEN REPORT. GREAT BRITAIN. DEPARTMENT OF EDUCATION AND SCIENCE. CENTRAL ADVISORY COUNCIL FOR EDUCATION (ENGLAND) (1967). *Children and their Primary Schools*. London: HMSO.

PORTER, S. (1979). *Problem Page*. London: Edward Arnold.

REASON, R. and BOOTE, R. (1987). *Learning Difficulties in Reading and Writing: A Teacher's Manual*. Windsor: NFER-NELSON.

REBAN, B. and POSTLETHWAITE, K. (1988). *Classroom Response to Learning Difficulties*. Basingstoke: Macmillan Educational.

ROSENBAUM, P., BARNITT, R. and LORNA-BRAND, H. (1975). 'A developmental intervention programme designed to overcome the effects of impaired movement in spina bifida infants'. In: HOLT, K.S. (Ed) *Movement and Child Development*. Clinics in Developmental Medicine. No. 55. London: Heinemann Medical for Spastics International Medical.

SCHOOLS COUNCIL (1978). *Startline*. Harlow: Longman Educational.

SHERIDAN, M. (1973). *Childrens' Developmental Progress From Birth to Five Years, The Stycar Sequences*. Windsor: NFER-NELSON.

SNOWDON WORKING PARTY. (1976). *Integrating the Disabled*. London: National Fund for Research into Crippling Diseases.

STOLLARD, J. (1988). *Children with Fine Motor Difficulties*, Gnosis 12. London: Diagnostic Centre for Learning Difficulties.

STOTT, D.H., MOYES, F.A. and HENDERSON, S.E. (1984). *Test of Motor Impairment*. Guelph, Ontario: Brook Educational Publishing.

TANSLEY, A.E. (1967). *Reading and remedial reading*. London: Routledge and Keegan Paul.

TOPPING, K. and WOLFENDALE, S. (1985). *Parental Involvement in Children's Reading*. London: Croom Helm.

WARNOCK REPORT. GREAT BRITAIN. DEPARTMENT OF EDUCATION AND SCIENCE (1978). *Special Educational Needs*. London: HMSO.

WECHSLER, D. (1949). *The Wechsler Intelligence Scale for Children*. New York: The Psychological Corporation.

WEDELL, K. (1973). *Learning and Perceptual-Motor Disabilities in Children*. Chichester: Wiley.

WOLFENDALE S. (1976). 'Screening and early identification of reading and learning difficulties. A description of the Croydon screening procedures'. In: WEDELL, K. and RAYBOULD, E.C. (Eds). 'Early Identification of Educationally "At Risk" Children', *Educational review*, Faculty of Education, Birmingham University.

WOLFENDALE, S. and BRYANS, T. (1987). *Handbook for Teachers, Perceptual Motor Training*. Stafford: NARE.

YOUNGHUSBAND, E., BURCHALL, D., KELLMER PRINGLE, M.L. (1970). *Living with Handicap: the Report of a Working Party on Children with Special Needs*. London: National Children's Bureau.

YUKER, H.E., BLOCK, R. and CAMPBELL, A. (1960). *A Scale to Measure Attitudes towards Disabled Persons*. New York: Human Resources Foundation.